ANN HILLYAR

Ann was born in Eltham, London, in 1938 and took up nursing at St Mary's Hospital, Paddington before marriage to a BP Oil executive with whom she had four children. She knew nothing of the psychical field and little of spiritual matters till both suddenly came upon her in 1980, when to her surprise she found herself part of events much later recounted by her new partner Jules Hillyar in his own book, *Between Heaven & Charing Cross*. She passed on in 2011.

EVERYMAN THE PILGRIM

ANN HILLYAR

First published in 2003 by
Amherst Publishing Limited
Longmore House, High Street,
Otford, Sevenoaks, Kent TN14 5PQ

Matador
9 Priory Business Park
Kibworth Beauchamp
Leicestershire LE8 0RX, UK
Tel: (+44) 116 279 2299
Fax: (+44) 116 279 2277
Email: books@troubador.co.uk
Web: www.troubador.co.uk/matador

ISBN 978-1783064-366

British Library Cataloguing in Publication Data.
A catalogue record for this book is available from the British Library.

Typeset in Aldine by Troubador Publishing Ltd
Printed and bound in the UK by TJ International, Padstow, Cornwall

Matador is an imprint of Troubador Publishing Ltd

This book is dedicated to our Teacher within it,
who never failed to show his hesitant pupils
love and patience.

THE BACKGROUND

Middle age is known to bring surprises – 'life begins' and so on. Much has been written on the subject of reaching forty, but few can have experienced the surprise that life sprung on me. What was this surprise? Did I find I was related to royalty, make an unlikely debut as an opera singer, sail up the Amazon? The foregoing I could have just about accepted, but to discover I was a trance medium took the wind out of my sails. To say I was amazed was an understatement.

Mediums to my mind dwelt in séance rooms, muttering cryptic words, with maybe a shawl or crystal ball thrown in for good measure. Hilarious episodes were recalled of having a flat in the house of a clairvoyant when newly married. Whispered requests of 'Is anybody there?' used to waft down to my basement rooms. Since the rent was cheap I cheerfully ignored such goings on. Yet years later, at the age of forty-two, as a negotiator for a firm of estate agents in a large Kentish town, divorced mother of four adult children – quite successfully as I saw it running my own life – I discovered I was one of 'these'. In my case, however, the popular image was not at all the reality.

It happened soon after I met Jules and was a turning point for him too. Since the age of sixteen his assiduous study of psychical and esoteric knowledge had precipitated him through a chequered history. He had been spiritual healer, teacher, group-leader, rescue-worker, even an eastern disciple, besides a variety of mundane occupations in between – still young in his early thirties, but a bit jaded and travel-worn when I came across him in 1980. If an acquired dislike of formal techniques and mistrust of organisations had not always made him a loner he was certainly one now, former associates having dispersed and the closest of these having recently passed on. He had a book to write about it all, though in another sense he was waiting for something. There was a gap to be filled. He thought it was the private centre for study he wanted to re-start.

He didn't then realise that it was the centre for renewal he had to re-start within himself. Head knowledge outweighed inner growth. He had to begin again more purely.

I didn't know this either at the time. Nor was I in a position to understand it from that secular world of mine, about to be turned inside-out, upside-down by the extraordinary experience of trance control itself – something quite outside my rather dogmatic ideas of time and space. We were chatting together one day when, totally unexpectedly, I dissociated and became for the first time 'overshadowed'. It felt the strangest of sensations, starting in a way which I learnt later is usual to trance sensitives.

As I sat there, familiar objects in the room began to blur in outline. I closed my eyes, feeling dizzy. 'Inside' my head I saw a tunnel, though perhaps a cone is more accurate, with the tail of it tapering off into the distance. At the end of the cone appeared a tiny figure. I had no idea whether it was a male or female. The figure came towards me, seemingly advancing up the cone, the head getting larger and larger until it seemed much larger than my own. The head seemed to pass right through into my skull just above my nose and hover close to my face, almost touching it but not quite. I couldn't make out any features clearly – I simply knew it had eyes, a nose and a mouth. I wasn't the slightest bit frightened, I do remember that: just extremely surprised.

The face pressed close to mine, and my vocal chords felt as if they were being tugged. I wanted to speak but felt embarrassed. What on earth was I going to say? My mouth opened almost involuntarily and I quickly closed it again. I had only known Jules a few weeks at this time and was reluctant to make a fool of myself in front of him. I remember finally making a decision to let the words form. I wasn't under any kind of coercion to speak. There was no feeling of 'must' or 'having to'. I seemed to enter into gentle agreement with the owner of the face to speak for him/her. Then:

'This is Michael,' my voice croaked. 'We have so much to say.'

Distantly I heard Jules answer, 'Welcome Michael,' but his voice seemed to come from behind a closed door.

The face 'melted' back inside my head. It was difficult to breathe. I felt a pressure on my chest, and the tops of my legs began to shake and tremble as if the muscles had been overexerted. My inexperience had forced him to withdraw. The encounter had not been a fearful one. In fact it filled me with curiosity, which in the gradual course of development over the next few years allowed through a large group of twenty-two discarnate workers having 'much to say' and do.

When those sessions began I thought that trance was going to be a lonely feeling. It seemed so at first. Even though Jules had spent most of his adult life sitting with sensitives, I nevertheless felt he could not really know what I was trying to describe. Many experiences in this world are, of course, common to all: ordinary, seemingly mundane events on which one can compare notes afterwards. This was DIFFERENT. This set one apart. This, one wanted to keep under wraps, feeling like a social pariah. And yet at the same time it was a matter of *hugging* the secret to oneself; not afraid, not disturbed, just wanting to examine it quietly and objectively.

I never dreamed that the depth and breadth of our long, fruitful association with these discarnates would unfold my heart like theirs in prayer for others; or that years later a radical refinement in my mediumship would see them introduce a special 'Unknown Communicator' for whom out of love and respect I would agree to share my secret, along with his diary of advice to Everyman on the spiritual path. Trance was left behind. I heard the Unknown Communicator clairaudiently and would transcribe his words onto paper.

But back there in 1980 with discarnate Michael, I was still 'wet behind the ears'. A couple of months of rather hesitant talks took place between the group he represented and us, via my tender mediumship. I had to adjust to the complete strangeness of the situation, and they had to accustom themselves to their new transmitter. Then, steadily, confidence increased on both sides. It became clear that they were descendants, so to speak, of those with whom Jules had been involved in rescue work a decade earlier, having sufficient know-how during our sessions to help him with that needed review of his, besides much else.

Realisation dawned on Jules and I that these discarnates were endeavouring to forge a strong bond between our two worlds. Respect for them grew as the seriousness of their purpose became apparent.

A calm, peaceful atmosphere is necessary for that purpose,

and one was provided. Within it we set aside an hour each Sunday and Wednesday evening; an hour of listening to contemplative tapes of words and music. As the tape finished I would feel a prompting to dissociate, or 'move aside' as it were, whereupon one or other of the group would talk to Jules answering questions on a wide range of subjects such as prayer, healing and general guidance. Jules was reviewing now with the heart.

Six years passed. A blow fell. I had Parkinson's disease diagnosed. When the illness began to take its toll I could no longer work at the estate agents. While my health progressively weakened the talks became more and more infrequent. Finally they stopped altogether. 'What next?' we asked ourselves.

A strong urge, a compulsion even, to live by the sea had been with me since childhood. We decided therefore to sell our house in Kent, glad to leave behind a town which had become grubby and commercial, and May 1988 found us settling to a new life in a Devon seaside environment. My fervent wish fulfilled, my health began to improve in the relaxing surroundings. Still no communications, although we kept faith twice a week as always, sensing our discarnate friends were with us. Another year passed however without any comment from them. Jules and I both felt a change of format was called for. Almost as a final resort we tried sitting in complete silence, putting away our music tapes.

The strangeness of it at first made me feel awkward; my stomach kept rumbling and extraneous thoughts wandered into my mind unbidden and unwelcome. But tension was released when halfway through I heard a subjective voice saying:

'Next time have pad and pen to hand.' Taking us with a

thrill of surprise, this fresh initiative on their part brought them more acutely into our life again.

Before these friends become silent attendants to the mainstream of dictation from the Unknown Communicator, I will refer to each of them by name, with short comments and views from some of them, which might help lessen the anonymity of a group we had got to know so well during the previous eight years.

Anyway, heeding their latest counsel, and somewhat intrigued, Jules and I kept our venue with them as usual, the required pad and pen now on my lap. This new phase of my mediumship was about to begin with adjustments necessary on both sides. Jules expressed his willingness to bow out should any future work only involve myself. Indeed, was it presumptuous of us to imagine both our further services were still called for at all? The date was May 31st 1989. David's voice startled me, speaking out loud. It sounded crisp and deep, and the suddenness of it made me jump.

'You are needed. You will benefit. Our new plan, which will unfold, includes you *both*. You have journeyed to us on your own. Well done.'

In ending the background to these sessions, I must explain that Jules and I sat in our rooms for about forty-five minutes prior to an eight o'clock start. My inclination was to use this private time for prayer, at some point during which I would be aware that the discarnates had arrived. Then Jules would join us, sensing their presence when he entered but unable to identify them individually. Neither could he hear them, relying upon my report at the end.

No attempt is made here to cover the long saga of evidence for the sources claimed, or indeed the doubts originally suffered and overcome. By the year in which the material for this book emerged we had become wholly satisfied in that respect and a bond of mutual confidence had established itself in the firm ground of tried and tested experience.

For now I will step back and allow the events of that fruitful year to unfold, trusting that the goodness of intent speaks through the words to follow. Only I can vouch for my integrity and humbly hope it will be accepted.

PART I

STARTING WITHIN

PRELIMINARY EXCHANGES

4th JUNE 1989 – Margaret and Persephone
Quietly sitting in my room beforehand as usual, knowing the two communicants above were already present, my mind was reflecting on David's words: 'You are needed, you will benefit,' when these thoughts were abruptly scattered by the arrival of an invisible intruder.

This was not one of our group of discarnate friends but an individual who has made himself known to me on a few occasions over the years. He can best be described as someone who likes to try his hand at 'putting a spanner in the works'. You may have had the pleasurable enjoyment of settling down to a train journey with two or three friends, anticipating a good chat with them, when into the compartment come a couple of youths looking for an opportunity to express anti-social behaviour to the detriment of everyone else's peace and quiet. We don't change into angels upon 'dying'; in fact our attitudes can stay very fixed. Every possible assistance for change is offered by guides and helpers. Not all welcome it, and my uninvited guest seems to fall into that category.

I had just sneezed, and the need for a tissue being imperative I stood up to fetch one from the dressing table behind my chair. Then quite literally I found myself knocked off balance, spun round and held face down over the back of the chair. I recognised the familiar tactics of my old adversary and made every effort with loving thoughts to calm him. These he summarily brushed aside, so I began to call to Jules in the next room for help.

After what seemed like an age, he finally heard my muffled voice and quickly came in. At once the intruder moved away, angry at his game being thwarted, and Jules pulled me to an upright position. A message was received from Persephone to pray for my attacker out loud, which I managed to do with some difficulty. He moved restlessly round the room for several minutes, then was gone.

Now why, you may be asking, did Persephone and Margaret not step in and help? For two reasons I think. First, earthbound discarnates, such as the one just described, tend to ignore helpers from a higher level, responding more easily to prayers from earth. Second, I had sufficient experience as a medium to cope with such situations. I had been lax about affording myself the necessary protection. Anyone praying for disturbed, distressed people whether incarnate of discarnate, should do so. After all, none of us would go to the Arctic without first insulating our physical body. Not surprisingly therefore I heard Persephone's mild reproof:

'Always surround yourself with a protective aura before going forth to pray for some souls. Forgetfulness on your part tonight has led you to a painful reminder. Sitting in the silence is good mental discipline for you both, although you do not have to concentrate on us all the time. Follow any line of thought that will carry you inwards and upwards.'

Suddenly came an objective picture of Margaret: a pleasant looking lady, early seventies, hair tied back from a wide face.

Jules followed with a question on some problems he was undergoing. He asked if it was considered wise in his case to use a professional hypnotist.

Margaret:

'This is an important question for you. Don't use outsiders. Let the solution come to you of its own free will. If you saw a hypnotist – unless you really trusted him – you would still resist releasing the block. He would be working from within the confines of a conventional training structure that would impede you.'

7ᵗʰ *JUNE, 1989* – Lawrence

The session began in quieter vein. Jules said he had suffered nightmares over the past few years, but always they had followed the same pattern, as if something was coming in through his bedroom window liable to crush him, or else feeling that heavy objects were falling on him. He would call out at the same time, then awaken distinctly uncomfortable and ruffled.

'Could whoever is here comment?' he asked.

Lawrence:

'There is a quite spontaneous resolving of this problem occurring at astral level. Once you ask for help, a chain of events begins to be enacted in which you need not take part.'

Jules was satisfied and somewhat relieved. During this, whether connected or not, I saw a woman with hair tied back in a bun, prominent veins standing out on her cheeks. She had a worried expression. My inability to recognise her didn't unduly surprise me for we knew that the Group sometimes brought people with them to our meetings. Occasionally others would 'look in on us' so to speak, just coming and going.

11ᵗʰ JUNE, 1989 – Christopher and Geoffrey
This session mentions two of my 'aspect selves', and as they are also featured further on in the dictations an explanation is needed for those to whom the term may be unfamiliar.

It was so to me, until understanding grew from personal trance encounters as well as discarnate teachings.

Our Higher Self or Soul sends out aspects or facets of Itself into various realities, both physical and nonphysical, in order to gain experience. The physical personality we know is one such aspect. Others remain in what we would regard as post-death realities, following their own way of existence. Some of these are our former incarnational selves who have carried on where we branched off, and some have never incarnated at all.

The complexities of aspect psychology* are not relevant to our text, but we are said to be part of a 'gestalt of consciousness', and that certainly seems to have been my experience.

Our link with another aspect's existence may make itself felt even though we may be totally unaware of its

_____

* see 'Adventures in Consciousness' by Jane Roberts. Prentice-Hall

independent life, as it is unaware of ours. You may experience a strong desire to become a musician, for example. Deep down inside you feel you could be a *good* musician. Many hours are spent in practice but fluidity of expression is elusive; you still seem mediocre. Now it is possible that the musical creativity so longed for is being achieved by another aspect self elsewhere. Your particular talents are nevertheless of vital importance for the 'all round' completeness sought by the Higher Self, showing themselves in ways that another aspect self cannot achieve. We all know how our daily thoughts, our daily moods and behaviour do affect people. But because we are so much more deeply internally linked with our aspect selves their moods affect us in a direct, intimate way.

Reluctant though I feel to describe my own aspect selves, revealed to me some four or five years ago, it seems necessary if only to emphasise how human, diverse and vulnerable can be their personalities.

Morris – who is an intelligent, taciturn man in his early thirties, constantly berating himself for his behaviour, which he feels lets him down. He once preferred to be entirely alone, pulling his hair and scratching himself in frustration. He frequently lapses back into his old ways.

Gerald – who is an old man, not well educated, who likes to live alone in his cottage with his collie dog, 'Peg-Leg'. He came to learn from the guidance of helpers how much he could benefit from the company of others, and so gradually 'opened' the door of his house, realising that one is in danger of atrophy if one totally excludes other people from one's life.

The knowledge of what it means to love another dawned on him after he had met Morris.

Josephine – who is a young, vivacious personality with curly auburn hair. She has never had an earth incarnation. She effected Morris's introduction to Gerald and likes to 'keep an eye' on their progress.

Ann – who is of course equally an 'aspect' self.

A certain lowness and depression over the past few days led me to enquire about Morris and Gerald, not having heard about them of late. I also asked whether the Group wished us to continue the sessions in silence, which we were finding quite difficult, or whether we should try a different approach. Geoffrey:

'Morris wanted to be by himself again, and has retreated to be near the wood. This could account for your somewhat heavy heart of late. Gerald is happy and outgoing, such a different person than when you first met.'

'To answer your second question: yes, we do wish you to continue in silence. As you are finding, it is a difficult discipline but one that is essential for you both. Don't worry if your thoughts keep wriggling like worms. Just centre yourself again, and gradually they (the thoughts) will come under your control.'

Jules then enquired what Seth (a discarnate teacher) meant when he talked about the 'feeling-tone'. He quoted direct: 'Your emotional feelings are often transitory, but beneath there are certain qualities of feeling uniquely your own, that are like deep musical chords. While your day-to-day feelings may rise or fall, these characteristic 'feeling-tones' lie beneath.' Jules felt he couldn't quite understand what was meant by the expression, and wondered too if he was blocking their discovery within himself.

Geoffrey:

'I think he means your own sense of real integrity, thoughts that match your unique inner deep core of reality. Practice creates an open channel so that the outer you becomes a true reflection of your inner self – like striking the right note of music on a piano, you know when you have hit the correct key. These quiet sessions will help you find the key.'

'Your anxieties are causing the block. Try the old, well-tested formula of writing down ALL that you are anxious about, and look at each statement carefully. Underline those that seem most important to you and then examine them again. Keep whittling them down. A freedom should be released if you are as honest with yourself as possible.'

14th JUNE, 1989 – Michael and 'H'

Due to outside noise from a neighbour building an extension to his house, I had been finding it difficult to concentrate during my private prayer time before eight o'clock. I asked for advice with the problem.

'H':

'Don't worry about trifles. Try to bring your thoughts up to the top of the skull. There will be a tight feeling around the forehead that will soon go.'

18th JUNE, 1989 – Paul and Duncan

Jules found the listing of anxieties rather unproductive and said so. He couldn't home in on the roots of his problem and found the effort rather fruitless.

Duncan:

'If Geoffrey's suggestion didn't work, then we are back to another of our favourite words – acceptance. Accept your tension, and carry it as a part of yourself for the time being. In other words, try to live with it as an old friend and just get on with your life. It seems a handicap but it doesn't have to be. It can be a great motivator; if it seems to be a part of you, leave it with you. Once you accept something it has a way of reducing in size and intensity. Or alternatively, use any method which seems to help you as an individual – however outlandish or extreme it may seem. You know YOU.'

21ˢᵗ JUNE, 1989 – Simon and James

Midsummer's day – hot, dry and still. Like most people Jules and I were spending more time out of doors than was usual for an English summer, writing and reading in desultory manner.

Jules was reading out loud when my lazy mood was jolted by the sudden picture of a large, pale blue eye regarding me sternly. The experience disturbed me, although it had only lasted for about half a minute, and my mind kept returning to it for the rest of the day. That evening I asked Simon and James if the eye had any connection with me, realising while asking the question that I felt strangely shy about the episode.

James:

'That was your Higher Self. You see him as a stern, rather remote figure, judging your every action and word. Indeed, you feel at times that it is impossible ever to be anything like him in behaviour. So you 'saw' in this way. He is young, about twenty-five, short, around 5'6" – 5'7" in height in your terms, with very fair hair swept back off his forehead and yes, he has pale blue eyes. He has a calm and gentle disposition. You may tell Jules that his Higher Self is a jovial, amiable man, again young, about thirty to thirty-two in your years. To help the personalities they have sent forth they take on earth guise, to make it easier for you to identify with them.'

I wasn't absolutely sure, but I thought James said that Jules' Higher Self had a beard. Their names were also made known.

A MYSTERY FIGURE ARRIVES

5th JULY 1989 – James and 'H'.
James spoke quietly to me while I was sitting in my room before the session.

'Listen. We want to tell you, to reassure you, that the manner in which you are both conducting these sessions is the right way for us. This is such a clear route for our approach. Tell Jules that his endeavours to follow Duncan's words on acceptance are beginning to bear fruit. It has the effect of unplugging his etheric, and the escape of poison leaves a cleanness and freshness within him. He is becoming more self-assured in important areas. He will know which ones. (Jules quietly entered at this point.) Tell him he does not disturb us coming in. He is indeed welcome.'

Jules opened with a prayer as usual, after which I heard nothing for about fifteen minutes. Then, subjectively, came James' rather robust voice breaking into song – a totally new occurrence.

He was singing the last verse of John Bunyan's famous hymn – 'To be a Pilgrim'.

'Since, Lord, thou dost defend

Us with thy Spirit,
We know we at the end
Shall life inherit.
Then fancies flee away!
I'll fear not what men say,
I'll labour night and day
To be a Pilgrim.'

Another pause of a minute or two. We waited, sensing a 'buzz' in the room. All of a sudden I knew that an entirely unfamiliar discarnate had joined James and 'H' – one whom I was certain I had not met before but whose presence was calm and reassuring. Gently he asked me to begin writing. What I can only describe as perfect trust surrounded me, although the way by which sentences flowed into my head was to me shrouded in mystery. They had a dreamlike quality about them.

'A pilgrim on the path, seemingly trite words and yet beautiful ones. Difficult too, for it is all too easy to stray. But the further you go the less you want to turn back. To believe in the companion who walks with you, eager to help you along, who will help you with the difficult, awkward bits, *that* is to have faith. And without faith you do not believe you will make it to the welcoming home that awaits you all. All are welcome and there is room for all. No one is ever turned away. No one need feel small or ashamed because without you the home could not BE.

'There would be so much comfort in your world if people could only believe this simple truth. So share your burdens, and help carry the load for your weaker brother. You will both get there in half the time! Goodnight.'

On that encouraging note, James, 'H', and the Unknown Communicator left the room.

9thy JULY, 1989 – Unknown Communicator
THE PILGRIM'S JOURNEY
U.C. continued his theme of the previous session: 'A pilgrim is one who journeys, who sets out with a goal in mind and yet is often not sure if he has the wherewithal to achieve his objective. You two are pilgrims and I know it has not always been easy for you, but it should be very much smoother for a while. Keep your eyes, ears, mind and heart very alert. Try also to be flexible and open. Many will depend on this, although they will not realise it, and nor will you to begin with. No need to think of it becoming an onerous responsibility. You are on a well worn path, but the more feet that can travel it, the clearer and more well defined it will become. It will be one of the major routes. Enjoy your journey on it. It should be light and easy. Goodnight.'

12th JULY, 1989 – David Wood (Jules' guide)
Jules asks whether the phrase 'try to keep flexible and open' applied as much to the sessions as to day-to-day living.
David:
'No more than at any other time. We do want you to feel free during the sessions to pursue any inner avenues you may wish to explore.'

J:

'David, if one senses that one has a wrong attitude without being able to get a grip on what that is, is it realistic to sometimes try laying open one's mind as if there was no attitude there at all – as though one had dispensed with an attitude altogether – and simply wait for it to be filled by a new one?'

D:

'You can, of course, try what you suggest but quite honestly I do not feel it would be realistic in your case. May I suggest reading would be of more help, particularly the books of either the ones you call Seth and Rajneesh, but more so those of the latter. Set time aside to *really* read and study them. You will be drawn to the right passages.'

16th JULY, 1989 – Unknown Communicator
THE MANY FACETS OF LOVE

> 'Love is unselfishness
> Awake in mens' minds,
> Love used all-seeing
> Can never be blind.
> Love used with gentleness
> Can set your heart free,
> Love used with strength
> Is all that you need
> To make you the pilgrim
> To help set man free.'

I had asked before the session for help with my physical problems as well as my emotional ones.

U.C:

'True faith, and your Guide
at your side,
Will bring you home
On the ebb of the tide.'

'Good-night.'

19th JULY, 1989 – James

The Unknown Communicator was again trying to express through me his theme of Love. However, I was not picking up the essential essence of what was being transmitted. So James suddenly said the following:

'I want to tell you a little of how we live.

'Our houses are small and simply furnished in soft, muted colours. These colours can be changed by just a thought to suit different moods. We have no need for speech. Thoughts pass between us on gossamer like strands. Our houses are built in a semi-circle on the side of a sloping hill. In the distance we can see where Co-Ordinator and Instructor live together in a low building made of creamy-coloured wood. This building houses ten people of whom they are but two. Our Group meets daily with Co-Ordinator and Instructor and from them we hear where on Earth is the greatest need for our work.

'A little way down the slope of the hill is our tiny chapel, a very simple building made of oak. It is round, about twenty feet in diameter, and our chairs are placed in a circle. In the middle of the circle is a round table, and on it we just have one wooden candlestick with a deep golden candle, which is always alight. One or two of us are always in the chapel, even when the rest are on a mission. There are seven windows with deep blue glass in them, very plain, but they reflect all the light and centre it on the candle. This helps to keep it constantly alight. The cloth on the table is plain gold coloured.

'We do not dress in robes, but in dark blue trousers and shirts, and on our feet are plain brown sandals. Margaret wears a dark blue dress. We find these garments easy to wear. Food is supplied from a central 'store' – mainly bread, cereals etc.

Many folk still like to ply the trade they had on earth – i.e. bakers and farmers. We only need one meal a day, though we still have personal preferences as we did when on earth – for instance some of us like more bread than others. I enjoy a cup of tea!

'We all like working in this close knit fashion, and any differences or friction have long since been ironed out. Mind you, we still have lively discussions – we are not a band of 'yes-men'. The climate is temperate but if we wish to experience again, say, a cold winter, it is perfectly possible so to do. Thought you might be interested in all this, Jules.'

23rd JULY, 1989 – Unknown Communicator
U.C:
'Michael did say right back at the beginning that there was 'much to say' so you were warned!

LOVE FROM THE UNENDING SOURCE

'Love is the hub of your planet. Of course, without it there would be no life in your terms. It continually wells up and flows over from the unending Source. Most do not even notice it, let alone begin to appreciate all it can mean to them. It comes unselfishly and yet is rejected thoughtlessly. It weaves its wonderful spell over and around every single person. But in the main it is brushed aside unheeded while people prefer to play with dross, with its tawdry imitations, fooling themselves that they have found the real thing, ignoring the fact that they have something of immense worth in their lives, which creates indeed their very existence.

'It can never disappear though, because there are always those amongst you who *know* the true golden value of love and who can spin it into their lives so a shine and a sparkle comes through them. Those who play and amuse themselves with the gaudy imitation know, deep down, when they see the real thing, and curiosity begins to niggle at them as to how this person came by this precious commodity. Then comes a gentle moment to talk a little of what it means to you to experience love. If we look hard into our lives we have all experienced it – although the expressing of it is hard I know. But always on your planet are those whose job it is to keep the golden threads of love brightly burnished. And we who have gone a little higher are grateful and salute your endeavours. How marvellous to be an earthly pilgrim. You know, I half envy you in a way.'

'Good-night.'

26ᵗʰ JULY, 1989 – Unknown Communicator
Jules apologises if, at any time, his questions may inadvertently interrupt U.C's train of thought.

U.C: THE SENSE OF FREEDOM

'No, don't feel that you have to say that. Feel free to speak whenever you want to, Jules.

'In saying this to you I want you to experience freedom during these times we spend together, and then carry this sense of freedom with you always. It is something to be infinitely treasured, to be cultivated, for with freedom you hold the key that will unlock your tension. Now what is this freedom? It is acknowledging to yourself your right for existence, for being – that you are part of the very pattern of Creation, an essential part.

While on earth this is so difficult to grasp – the fact that you are needed here at this precise moment in time. This idea of freedom gives you all the tools you need to *carve your niche.*

'As the outer covering loosens up you give the Higher Self an opportunity to experience. You still all make prisons out of your mistakes and human failings. Your cell, your prison, has no door clanged shut however. Freedom is there and you can walk free any time *you* wish it. Sometimes the confines of your self-made prison seem almost comforting, although your eyes and thoughts dart wistfully and longingly to those who have set themselves free. Everyone has the God-given right to walk free at any time. I, and many like me, are always at hand to help.

'So talk away to me – either out loud or in private. You must never think you are interrupting. And don't forget:

everyone has this right to explore, to exist, to make mistakes, to fall down, and to get up again. What a journey we are all on, Jules, one of great exploration!

'Good-night.'

30ᵗʰ *JULY, 1989* – Unknown Communicator

Jules was in his room for this session as his back was painful and he couldn't sit up. This particular evening, as luck would have it, I was feeling tense and nervy; emotions not helped by the fact that I was having to sit on my own – an unusual occurrence. The lonely sensation began to be dispelled by U.C's dictation.

U.C: THE PATHWAY

'Words we often use, referring to the link between ourselves and earth, are 'the pathway' or 'the bridge'. These words create an artificial division in your mind, which I would like to narrow, for in real terms the division does not exist. When I tell you that you are a 'pathway or a bridge', I sense your discomfiture. Nevertheless I reiterate the words and will try to explain them.

'You are flexible, co-operative and submissive. I don't mean of course that you have no will of your own, (literally God forbid), but that you are learning the wisdom of sublimating the wants and wishes of the lower self to the Higher Self. In so doing your chakras are beginning to align, thereby allowing me, and others like me, to operate closer to earth. You are forging a 'pathway'. We can look through a tube that has no obstructions, if that is a clearer explanation. This is painful for you at times because the lower chakras have to be opened and cleansed to match up to the higher ones. Work is being done by you as well as by us to widen your lower chakras; so do not be surprised if you feel raw and edgy.

'Often during this purifying operation the personality catches glimpses of its Higher Self and feels ashamed of being seen. Don't be. He chose you for this particular experience and cares about you. However, you can keep the overcoat smart, and that way you will feel more comfortable. What I am talking about does not apply to you alone, but to every single person. Everyone can become a channel for his Higher Self, and indeed everyone eventually will. I know it requires discipline and self awareness, which sound tough on their own, so I would add liberal sprinklings of the following: laughter, love, a sense of adventure, and creativity. Especially creativity as, after all, what are you helping to create but your own Soul!'

'Good-night.'

His final remark reminded us that, while the Soul or Higher Self is very much a stable individual already in existence, it is also said to be in a continual state of 'becoming' or 'unfoldment' through the creative experience of its aspect selves.

2nd AUGUST, 1989 – Unknown Communicator
A woman known to us was being evicted from her home of twenty years for nonpayment of rent – a traumatic emergency for her, culminating in a scene which Jules subsequently happened to witness. Although at that specific point tears came to his eyes on her behalf, overall he was surprised to

21

find, in a moment's true self-observation, that his sympathy lay only on the surface.

He had until then considered himself a kind enough 'everyman', often happy to go out of his way to assist people when necessary. Therefore, it came as something of a revelation to discover how skin-deep were his feelings in such a case. 'A lack of heart,' he confessed dejectedly.

U.C: REBUILDING THE PERSONALITY

'I am glad that you felt able to express what you did because that truly is the first step on the road to freedom.

'Acknowledging what you really feel, seeing yourself in a naked, harsh light, no pretending, no games – that is the next step. Once you are stripped down to the bare bone, then another 'you' will begin to emerge. You have a half-formed picture in your mind of the sort of person you would really like to be. I know you have suffered a few sharp shocks just lately about the old you and feel that the time has come to discard him. Well then, this half-formed picture will become clearer to you, that I promise, and another step of freedom will be taken.

'You naturally have to have a personality for your life span, but you do not have to be stuck with the one you have. You are ready now for major changes. You have imagination, and an agile, fertile mind; plus you have a deeply grained sense of what is right. You have reached a stage of self-disgust where to live with yourself as you are creates discomfort. You have a great respect of justice and fair play, and these two characteristics combined will enable you to rebuild your personality into someone of whom you can be justly proud –

another step towards freedom. Freedom means not having to continually worry about your behaviour, but you have been trying to change without taking off all your old clothes. Once stripped then it is your choice what the new outfit will be.

'I will talk to you again about this. We do meet in sleep life but it doesn't matter at all that you can't remember on waking.

'Good-night.'

6th AUGUST, 1989 – Unknown Communicator
Jules thanked U.C. for his pertinent remarks last time, which had been encouraging. He added, however, that although he had tried to be more conscious of his true feelings, he usually only experienced a blankness – as if truth had found itself about to be watched and cunningly jumped behind him.

U.C: THE EMERGENCE OF THE NEW PERSONALITY
'Don't worry about the blankness. An analogy I could use is to think of the old cinema screen, when there was always a pause between one slide and another. Nothing appeared on the screen.

'Referring back to our last talk, Jules, remember what I said about you being ready for major changes. Quite naturally during this period there will be blankness. As I said, a new personality will emerge but you have not yet got the measure of him. He is slowly taking form, taking on flesh and blood, waiting in the wings for you to 'take him on board'. You don't need me to tell you that at the moment you are a head person. This new personality will be a much more balanced head and heart man. You will suffer rebuffs as you make overtures with the heart, but everyone does. Try not to let that disturb your newly acquired poise. You see, the blankness will soon have movement, design and colour. The heart has to open slowly to avoid distortion. Yours has been tightly shut for some length of time so freedom will creep in cautiously. One suggestion to help you with the heart problem: remember how you felt as a child – what gave you pleasure, what made you cry, what stirred you. Childhood remembrances can be most helpful. You are finding freedom, too, through writing.

'Good-night.'

9th AUGUST, 1989 – Unknown Communicator
The residue of our affair with that evicted acquaintance was churning around in my mind when I took to my room for the customary quiet time. My sympathy had given her a shoulder to cry on, and an afternoon's 'open house' was supplied to the whole family.

But a monetary gift to cover the fuel bill was later found to have been carelessly tossed aside. The same attitude was also applied to her six cats, whose resultant, starving state had saddened me.

Being particularly fond of cats I had begun to feed them as best I could on the understanding that she would resume responsibility for them herself within a couple of days after the eviction. Two days had stretched into five. This afternoon had found another lady and myself attempting to round up the pitiful creatures so that the Cat Protection League could try to find them homes.

The whole episode had cut me to the quick. I truly

thought that she cared for her pets, and her subsequent rejection of them only served to emphasise my own feelings of having been used and let down.

U.C: SUNSHINE DISPELLING SHADOWS

'Try to see everyone as reflections of the Christ light. Now don't cry. I am sitting beside you, right here with you. Don't be afraid to use my strength. Listen to me. When a shadow falls over another person, it is not of course the Christ light receding but your own shadow lengthening, causing an eclipse of the light. You have it in you to walk always in sunshine, to see everything that happens as a gift from God. The sunshine in you *will* dispel the shadows. The warmth of your sunshine will shorten another's shadow, and this can only be good. No action is ever wasted, even those that seem futile – especially those, I may add, that do seem futile if the idea behind it springs from service.

'David is here with me tonight and I know he wishes to say something.'

'Jules, this may surprise you but you really have come a long way over the past two years. At last you want to change. Don't worry if any suggestions we make don't work for you. Live your life as fruitfully and wisely as you can. Let anger, frustration, boil out of you quickly, cleanly. Don't hang on to it. Squeeze out every drop. Very soon you will tire of this particular emotion, and feel much, much fresher in your approach to small, irksome problems. U.C. says 'Good-night,' and I say 'God bless you.'

13th AUGUST, 1989 – Unknown Communicator

Jules said that he had been trying to become aware of his true feelings as had been suggested. And whatever the truth may be, he saw his own belief that he was good for nothing, unworthy of what he felt to be the rare, privileged light of their attention, guilty that he should be getting it, afraid that he might not match up to their expectations, and that as a result they, and/or David, would give up and go. He saw his feeling that Ann was all along of more service in prayer and as a heart-loving channel, and that he himself was just a worthless adjunct to the sessions. He saw his shame. It was the first time he had been conscious of these beliefs.

U.C: A STEP FOR FREEDOM

'You don't realise how truly glad I am that you felt able to express yourself so freely and honestly as you have just done. David will never leave you: no one is ever left without a guide. And we certainly won't be suddenly taking off. You see, you speak for Everyman, and when these discourses come eventually to be published, (as they surely will), your thoughts, your expressions of guilt, your natural apprehension as to whether you will match up to the 'new you' as we see him – these words will help and comfort many; because many feel just as you do – 'unworthy in the sight of God' I suppose it could be phrased. However, they feel unable to put their feelings into words, or have no one, as they see it, to say the words to. Then suddenly to pick up a book, and see written down, in question and answer form, anxieties, guilts etc., that have been oppressing them will give relief, will bring freedom.

So you can see perhaps how you are being of service and are much needed as a part of the team. What must seem to you like exclusive 'AI' attention therefore will eventually become far from exclusive to you but answers for many perplexed minds.

'Ann finds service through prayer and mediumship. Not many can work in this way. She has trained through many lives for it. But you are giving service in a different way. Speak to us, express how you feel whatever the emotion. Your honesty is stripping you bare now.

You are vulnerable but not, I repeat *not* alone. You are the true Pilgrim stepping out on the path, and as you journey you will begin to feel more assured of whom you are becoming, who this new person is. You have tonight made another step for freedom.

'Good-night.'

16ᵗʰ AUGUST, 1989 – Unknown Communicator
Jules said that his query last time had been fully answered by the prospect of the book. However, he didn't understand David's advice to 'let anger and frustration boil out quickly and cleanly'. Where do you let it out? This morning it had not even been directed at Ann, yet she had to leave the room feeling sick – as a sensitive would. To let it out into a pillow he knew from experience was useless, as the pillow was not the object of the anger. Also, anger remains even when it has boiled over. It continues boiling for some while. So what to do? Previous to the session he had tried to become aware of, or 'acknowledge the true feeling' behind his anger and frustration, and he thought it was something to do with feeling

unsafe basically. It was only a glimpse, but a picture came of sitting in a rowing boat, which was rocking dangerously with him holding onto the sides. He wondered if U.C. would care to comment.

U.C: LIVING WITH ANGER

'To take the questions you ask about your anger and David's response to you. Now, first of all, David is your guide because you and he have been good friends through several lives and you both share many of the same fine qualities, such as loyalty, and a strong desire to see a job carried through in the correct manner. However, the emotion of anger is one he has learnt to deal with, and he can only endeavour to help you in the same manner that *he* came to terms with it. This learning process for the main part took place while he was here, where emotions have to be more acutely brought under control. The phrases, the words he used, were part of a lesson that had been passed on to him by his Teacher.

'Ann, too, has learnt to control anger, and therefore also cannot be of much help to you with this particular problem. It has become diluted in her make-up.

'Now me: I was what you would call, I suppose, a firebrand on earth. But, as you have learnt painfully, the fire of anger burns and hurts and cannot seem to be extinguished.

'It is there all the time, but can be lived with on a more comfortable level. I threw myself into a cause. You can make your book throb and pulsate with exciting energy. Half the time we are angry about ridiculously small things. Indeed, the very triteness of them seems to cause even more irritation.

Surface irritations usually subside; deeper resentments have to be accepted as a part of one's psyche.

'To go on to the second part of your question: you will be feeling 'rocky' and edgy at the moment – transition from one stage to another will create this. You don't need me to tell you that most of your anger is directed against your own shortcomings. As the 'new man' takes shape you will feel calmer. Both of you need to keep a good sensible sense of perspective, and not let problems grow much larger than they really are. Keep the humour on the boil.

'Good-night.'

20th AUGUST, 1989 – Unknown Communicator
Poetry I have to confess is most definitely not my favourite art form, prose having preference in reading material. Imagine therefore my reaction this evening when I realised that U.C. was indicating again his wish to dictate another poem. All I knew was that the title was 'Coasts'. My hand was guided to write in the heading and the writing had a bold flourish to it, which is very different to my own rather cramped style. The poem was composed as he went along and took him about twenty minutes to complete.

U.C: COASTS

'From coast to coast
the Word will spread,
and ease each aching heart from dread.
The dread of loneliness and pain

will be transmuted by the Word.
The Word each heart will set aflame;
And Love, the winged messenger, set free,
Will proudly bear the torch on high
from coast to coast.

'Love, put into action through thought, can spread from coast to coast, making an instantaneous pathway that would amaze you if you could see it in action. Every loving thought sent out can reach a weaker brother, and strengthen his aura. If you could see this clairvoyantly, you would see his aura flash with a fire of gold and blue. These colours would permanently stay within his aura, whatever other emotions were raging through him at the time. You, too, would be strengthened; so think how much could be gained, and all by just a thought!'

'Good-night.'

23rd AUGUST, 1989 – Unknown Communicator
Jules said that he had appreciated the poem last session, focussing with slight difficulty on just two bits: 'The Word', and 'Love, put into action through thought'. He finally assumed 'The Word' meant the truth of being attuned to the Source, which is love. But putting love 'into action through thought' he had found was impossible whilst clouded inside with bitternesses, resentments, fears, and guilts etc. These felt so distinctly uncomfortable that one often longed for that universal panacea of Being. He believed such attainment to be necessary and inevitable, but 'The Word', the action, seemed way 'up there' and not 'down here'.

U.C: PEACE THROUGH DISCIPLINE

'Man on the long, twisting path of evolution, has to face himself; and I really do mean *face* himself. Not look at himself from 'down there' or sideways, but look straight at himself.

'To use an analogy: imagine your two selves, i.e. the Higher and lower as say members of the same battalion within an army. The lower self is a Private, and the Higher Self is a Colonel. Each has a respect for the position of the other. But the Colonel is very much in command, and the Private knows this. However, because of the respect he holds for the higher rank, he wants to come under its discipline. He enjoys the training, the setting aside of his own wishes and desires, and knows that his control will not only aid his senior officer, but ultimately the whole battalion. As you 'fall into line' you are helping others to 'keep in step'. So no 'down here' or 'up there', but face to face, a team working together with the junior member very much aware of the need for discipline: always checking that he is ready for orders. A long analogy I know, but one that may help you to form a picture in your mind.

'I can only say that you have to be ready to bite off words that long to be said, check thoughts that enter the mind unbidden. Slowly at first, and then with accelerating pace, rather like the raw recruit, the astral body comes to accept, even to welcome, the discipline. As you rightly said, bitter and resentful thoughts lead one to feel distinctly uncomfortable. I am not going to say it is easy. You know only too well it is not, and so do I. Oh yes, I found this particular lesson very hard, having had a quick and fiery temperament. At the same time it *has* to happen, and of course ultimately does. Probably

I risk sounding like an advertising slogan when I say – 'Peace is there for the taking.' Need I say more?

'Good-night.'

27th AUGUST, 1989 – Unknown Communicator

About five minutes before the session started at 8 p.m., I asked a question of U.C. relating to human love and the deep attachment I felt for my daughter, Catherine, who had been staying for a few days. To my surprise U.C. began dictation immediately.

U.C:

'Family attachments, if practised unselfishly are – or can be – a strong positive way of putting God's love into action. Unpossessive, unselfish, detached human love is one of the first steps on the Way. For without having★ experienced human love, you cannot begin to be aware of the enormous sacrifice that God makes for you in His unfailing giving, which reaches you through the loving aid of countless helpers.'

★U.C. had just begun the third sentence of the above answer when Jules entered. U.C. 'knew' that Jules would have one or two questions to ask, so stopped dictating. After the prayer Jules asked two questions. U.C. paid careful attention; then he made me draw a line across the page, about two or three lines below our half-finished sentence. He considered Jules' questions, half formulated a reply to the first, decided the second would require a longer, more detailed response and then took me back to the reply to my question. This reply finished exactly above the drawn line. Then he turned to Jules, his demeanour and style of delivery changing – becoming crisper, each word deliberately considered.

Jules was very thankful for the clear analogy of the Colonel and the Private. The trouble was he couldn't seem to hear any orders! However, it was good to have confirmed from U.C. the need to bite off words, control thoughts etc. which had more final and definite impact than those imbibed from other sources. Did this mean then, that Seth's advice – to alter one's basic *attitude* by getting behind false psychological beliefs, especially the 'core belief,' and dissolving same – was not applicable here? The advice to 'cull' negative thoughts seemed relatively superficial.

U.C: FOLLOWING THOUGHTS TO THEIR SOURCE

'Now to turn to you, my dear friend. First answer: all I can add is that the Private has to be attentive, on his toes, ready to respond, listening. In your own way you can attempt to do the same thing – trying to identify the Real from the unreal because the lower self tries to cajole with sweet words of distraction, endeavouring to obliterate the voice of the Higher Self.

'Answer to your second question. Seth is *so, so right* in urging and encouraging one to begin to identify one's core beliefs.

Of course, the very word 'core' emphasises how deep-seated they are, how difficult to isolate and *really* understand. However, it is perfectly possible. It will take a good deal of time, but is worth every minute spent on the task. You were, indeed still are feeling uncomfortable, tense etc. What I was giving you was an 'outer' exercise to try to help give some relief for your immediate problems. If you can begin to bite off the harsh words, or check the unpleasant thoughts, you should begin to feel calmer. Feeling calmer should help you to follow thoughts through to their source. Using the analogy of a maze: they can find their way back by the clear route, and not stray off down routes that have been clogged by obstacles composed of stale material of which you have become heartily sick. Working with your core beliefs should then be easier. You are also meeting resistance from two of your re-incarnational aspects, in regard to your strong wish to change. You are more developed than they, and therefore can alter your beliefs *if you so wish it.*

'Good-night.'

30ᵗʰ AUGUST, 1989 – Unknown Communicator
Severe pains around the crown chakra greeted me on waking this morning. Despite taking several Panadol, plus Jules giving me a head massage, the pain persisted. Indeed, by the time I came to sit in my bedroom around 7 p.m. it really was quite severe. It went in waves down to my right eye and then back to the crown. I requested healing and slowly it receded to a more acceptable level. U.C. being present by this time, I took the opportunity to ask him how to accept pain. Once again, as in the last session, he began immediate dictation, halting after the word 'Supreme' as Jules entered. Once more he took me back to the reply after listening to the prayer, Jules' questions, and making mental notes of his own answers.

U.C: A POSITIVE APPROACH TO PAIN
'Pain, correctly faced, can be a way of controlling the

mind, of helping to bring it under the sway and gentle dominance of supreme love. Pain can bring release of in-built tensions, so don't fight it. Rise up and down with the waves of it, just as you would gently bob up and down in the waves of the sea, enjoying the sensation.'

Jules said that U.C's points had been taken, the message received and understood. 'Harsh words and unpleasant thoughts', however, were out before one could say 'No', and more self-effort was needed. The news of resistance to this from two of his re-incarnational aspects only made him more determined. 'I *will* change,' he said, whether they like it or not. After all, 'the Colonel' is on my side in this regard. Therefore, to do so I *will* try harder.'

U.C:

'Yes, Jules, 'the Colonel' – or Higher Self – will be welcoming the words you have just uttered. To hear such words said will bring him joy, and he will help you all he can. He knows how hard is the struggle; for human life seems to be continually setting traps to snare the unwary. Once one small hurdle is achieved, the next will seem just that little bit easier.

'It may seem to you at first that you are having to work extra hard; not only on your own account, but also for those two recalcitrant aspects! However, rather like naughty children, they have had a surfeit of indulging themselves and will welcome gentle discipline and a more moderate diet. They will respond to you, as you are trying to do to 'the Colonel'. They are ignorant, by the way, of this person, so you will have a chance to open their eyes a little. Rather a turnabout for you Jules, as I know you have strived to open the minds of folk on earth to the fact that consciousness continues after bodily death. I don't suppose you ever imagined that you would be educating the minds of those with whom you have such a close involvement. The thoughts, emotions, feelings of one's other aspects are continually drifting in and out of one's own consciousness, *and* vice versa.

'The stronger personality can help the weaker, as I mentioned in a recent talk. I said if you help to carry the load for a weaker brother, you will both move more quickly along The Way. Don't let the responsibility weigh too heavily on you – it needn't at all. It is a privilege.

'Good-night.'

THE WAY

3rd SEPTEMBER, 1989 – Unknown Communicator
Jules said that U.C's answer last time was absolutely 'on the button', interesting and helpful. He felt quite able to 'carry' the other recalcitrants, though unfortunately had not yet come to regard this as a 'privilege'. Could he have an example of how their thoughts drifted into his? For it seemed that all his thoughts and feelings were to and from his *present* environment. Also, having settled very comfortably in the latter, he was aware of private fears that increased effort on his part might lead to further and greater 'tests' involving, possibly, a threat to that happy settlement. Would 'the next hurdle' really seem easier?

Before the session began, I had been talking to U.C. about 'The Way', and how it seemed so difficult at times, and also how hard it was to spot the difference between the voices of the lower and Higher selves. This was his answer:

'Try to hear only the real, true voice. You can tell the difference if you listen properly. To do so means first learning to recognise, then exercise, your higher motives as against the lower ones. Why do you want to walk the Way? It isn't easy.

37

It is continually beset with problems. And yet, despite everything, you have no wish to halt the journey. Why is this? Many do stop. Deep inside, however, you *know* that the goal will bring true happiness. Once all the material, tempting fruits of earth have been sampled and tasted, the appetite becomes jaded. You have now discovered that prayer and contemplation are *real* food, and nothing else will suffice. A gentle diet of these precious foods will give you all the strength you need for that walk on the Way. Your increased sense of what is the highest, what is right, real and true will draw you closer to that level and enable you to differentiate it more clearly. As you move along, your step will quicken in anticipation, like hastening homewards on a cold winter's night and in the distance glimpsing your house aglow with light.'

Before U.C. began his reply to Jules's first question, he asked Simon, who was present, to supply details about one of Jules's reincarnational selves, as he (U.C.) did not have any specific details about him. I could 'hear' Simon's voice in the background filling in the relevant information.

U.C:

'Right – into the first question, Jules. One of your reincarnational selves was interested in the idea of communicating with his companions through words. At the time he was on earth not many could read or write, but he had been quite well educated at home by his mother. He was therefore rather skilful and fluent in these arts. He had a quick, inventive mind, and realised that words, both written and spoken, could powerfully reach and influence many. In the latter half of his life he became caught up in religion, and made quite a name for himself as a preacher. I am communicating slowly to Ann about this fellow because the information is being supplied by Simon. You are not a preacher –far from it – but you are interested in sensible, logical communication. Your 'R.S.' still tries out phrases he might, or indeed did use, and you often half pick these up in small snatches, and convert them into modern day English. Does this help you to see what I mean about his thoughts drifting in and out of your consciousness?

'To take up your next point. You will doubtless be faced with one hurdle after another; everyone is. But they are never raised so high that you can't clear them. You have it in you to positively make all the effort required. Certainly put aside all ideas of calamities befalling you; the Divine Law does not work like that. Indeed, your effort will always bring its own reward.

'Good-night.'

6ᵗʰ SEPTEMBER, 1989 – Unknown Communicator
Dictation started by U.C. before the session began as usual at 8 p.m.

KINDNESS
'Kindness seems a very overused word for a little used deed. Yet it is easier in fact to be kind than harsh and acerbic. Kind words, kind thoughts, kind deeds, can touch, and often alter, another's way of looking at life. In turn they pass it onto the next person and so on.

'A whole community can be changed in this way. Harsh, thoughtless words not only hurt another, but bite deep into your own psyche, causing one misery and discomfort. Kindness can be likened to sunshine and warmth; harshness to cold east winds and greyness. I know which I would rather have!'

Jules was grateful for the trouble taken with the 'R.S.' example. He thought it particularly well put, and he now understood. But everything inside seemed so deep relative to the surface where he felt himself to be most of the time. Irritability, for instance, seemed to come from somewhere behind him, rushing past him into action before he could begin to control it. He felt bewildered in the middle at such times, helpless and almost in despair at ever being able to catch the emotion before it did damage. He realised of course that only he could do it, and wasn't expecting a miracle transformation. But could U.C. comment?

U.C: CHECKING ROGUE THOUGHTS

'You are the one in control. You *are* the one in control. As you say, no one can do this for you. Your thoughts are continually running along a well-worn track – a track which has become so smooth and highly slippery as to become dangerous. I use the word 'dangerous' to illustrate how easy it is to allow thoughts to slide away from you. A rogue thought is like a runaway train; but *you* are in the signal box, and can throw the lever over at the last moment, thereby avoiding a collision course. To start with, the levers will seem stiff, but gradually you will know when to apply them. Soon the thoughts will be sent down the right tracks, and the dangerous, slippery route can remain closed. I know it sounds tedious, but the checking has to be done over and over again. But you will be the benefactor in the long term; you, and your reincarnational selves.

'As I said to Ann last time, the Way is not easy but it is so well worth the effort. Your feet have to be set on it at some time. They want to tread that Way now, but something is preventing them. Is it this fear you were mentioning last time of calamities befalling you? Whenever you feel ready, *and only then,* we can pull these bogeys out of the bag and examine them. This may help you to break them down. Just let me say that you are being helped, and your efforts have not gone unnoticed. You have so much goodness in you, which is being overshadowed by carelessness. Your sense of humour often saves the day!

'Good-night.'

10th SEPTEMBER, 1989 – Unknown Communicator
Jules said that he liked U.C's words to Ann on kindness. He couldn't as easily relate, however, to the analogy U.C. had given about a rogue thought being like a runaway train, with oneself in the signal box quite able to throw the lever over at the last moment. In practice it was more a case of that train suddenly rushing past the signal box as if from nowhere, leaving no chance of levers being thrown. How do you know a thought until you've thought it? The analogy seemed more applicable to the *verbal expression* of thought, the restricting of it, which is as far as Jules had got. Also, in answer to U.C's question as to

what prevented the treading of The Way, Jules felt himself to be such a tangle of tension, guilt and carelessness etc. that feelings of unworth, unreadiness, were probably more deeply etched than any fear of 'calamity' tests to be undergone.

U.C: Service

'As you are stopping or controlling the rogue thought from being formed into words – words which may hurt – then this is an important step for you. By taking this step you are performing a service for your fellow man. This knowledge, that you can stop the thought from being expressed, should give you a feeling of confidence. It is this confidence in yourself that you so badly need at the moment. You need to feel of worth.

'I will now move onto your stutter, your speech impediment. On the surface this is greatly exacerbated by careless thoughts being translated into words. It is not your true voice – one that can express integrity, dignity, grace – that speaks these careless, stumbling words. However, if the thoughts are stopped and rearranged, it gives you, *the true you*, time to say in a dignified, kindly way exactly what you wish to communicate. So, not only are you performing a service for your fellow man, but an even greater one for yourself. As you move further along The Way, then your thoughts will be formed at source in an orderly fashion, and I do think your stutter will be *completely* eradicated in time.

'I will stop here because Ann is poorly tonight, but we can continue this theme again.

'Good-night.'

13th SEPTEMBER, 1989 – Unknown Communicator
I had been feeling frustrated this evening because I seemed unable to help a friend of ours with his personal problems. I decided to consult U.C. and he dictated the following reply.

U.C: A DIFFERENT ANGLE ON 'HELPING PEOPLE'

'An answer for your quandary about helping people as you describe it.

'Somebody may discuss with you a problem they are experiencing, and you have no instant answer. Quite frankly, how can you? However, you feel the need to proffer advice, ideas etc. You decide to write to your friend, who reads the letter several times. Nevertheless, he may decide he cannot put the advice you give into operation *at that precise moment*. But, *at that precise moment,* one of his aspect selves may be in need of just the sort of advice suggested for a problem of *his* own. The problem may not – probably won't be – known under the same circumstances as your friend's. But the friend may have been prompted by his aspect to seek help for himself.

'This may sound somewhat complicated but do you follow what I am getting at? You may not always be able to help someone you know on earth, but a generous response may give aid to one of his aspect selves. Never think a desire to help, to love, ever falls on barren ground.'

Jules said that the last session's words made a good deal more sense, were encouraging, and sounded workable. It only remained for him to make them so. He was impressed by the detailed helpfulness of U.C's suggestions, which were of a kind he had not yet seen in print, let alone from a discarnate source. If U.C. wished to continue the theme this session he would be most welcome to do so, in which case a further question in Jules mind needed only a yes or no answer. The question related to that 'person waiting in the wings' within him. Ideal images were forming already as to the required character and behaviour of such a person, but would these images be blocking the actual (and perhaps more realistic) nature from entering in?

U.C: (Addressing Ann again.)

'Child, we have much to do together. I will be able to guide you, to show you how to work behind the scenes with suicides, drug addicts, the bereaved, any whom society seems to reject.

'Jules, to return to you, my friend. No, in a nutshell, your imagined images of the new person 'waiting in the wings' cannot prevent him from approaching. To elaborate: he is there, he always has been there, through all your earth incarnations. The blueprint is formed. However, if you exercise your imagination to include him in your highest thoughts, then well and good. You want to change your way of approaching life's irksome problems, your old habits of thinking. Good again, because this begins imperceptibly to draw you closer to him. Slowly, and not I know without considerable tussle and effort on your part, you will merge into him. This amalgamation will mean that you will be thinking and speaking as he does; so no stutter of course.

'You will even appear to look taller, tension will be lessened so less stiffness in your muscles. Once again I reiterate, that I can see improvement in your attitude since we began these discussions three to four months ago. I like

44

your questions; they are clearly put and provide me with a challenge to give a concise answer.

'Good-night.'

17ᵗʰ SEPTEMBER, 1989 – Unknown Communicator
As I sat alone before the session, unaware of any presence with me, the following prayer came into my mind:

'Lord, help me to use words wisely, to speak sparingly, to speak truthful words, to speak healing words, to speak words of encouragement, to speak words of gentle humour, to speak words of love.'

Jules felt encouraged by U.Cs last explanation. Just one query remained about this 'person in the wings', who was described as 'always' having been there through all earth incarnations. At first this sounded to Jules like the soul or Higher Self. Dare he think it could be *him* that was 'waiting in the wings'? Yet U.C. had further said: 'The blueprint is formed.' That didn't sound like the soul. So was this mysterious person the astral self, or the soul's idea of what he wanted Jules to be? Was this the soul's blueprint for Jules, the lower self?

U.C: HOW THE BLUEPRINT IS CHOSEN

'This person 'waiting in the wings' is, as you say, the blueprint your Higher Self would like you to become in this incarnation. When I stated that he has been there through all your earthly incarnations, this is also the case. As each soul grows and develops, he sends out to earth, with ever increasing intensity, the personality that is to garner fresh experience for him. There is a blueprint for the personality. The blueprint is discussed and drawn up at case conferences; this is, of course, before that particular personality's emergence onto the earth scene. The case conference members are usually made up of the Higher Self (or soul); the head of the Group Soul composing the tier at that time; the guide chosen as most suited to work with the personality; a Higher Being such as the one you call Co-ordinator. He would be present because the experiences to be gathered are not just for that particular soul alone, but to enrich the whole Group Soul.

'As you know, the soul has to experience many different kinds of incarnations. It has small, seemingly insignificant ones to start with, and then more exacting ones. But always there is the blueprint – even for the early, more primitive type of incarnation. Just as the first car to be manufactured was relatively simple in design and now is highly complicated, so the same can be said for incarnations. Machinery does not operate very efficiently if the blueprint for its design is not carefully followed and it is the same for the personality. You are beginning to get glimpses of how comfortable it is to operate efficiently. You seem to be aware when you are not matching the blueprint. This awareness is *good*, is *important*.

'Good-night.'

FREEDOM AND MEDITATION

20th SEPTEMBER, 1989 – Unknown Communicator
Jules said that the explanation about the blueprint suddenly lit up the 'person in the wings' with meaning. It felt more realistic, even enticing, to match the Higher Self's blueprint for him than to attempt any match with the Higher Self. Although he was increasingly aware that he didn't match the blueprint at all, he accepted his awareness as being good. He was also aware that he didn't experience the quality of 'freedom' U.C. wanted to encourage in these sessions, and it left him unsure which mental posture to adopt out of the many available to him in this forty minutes, especially now that meditation seemed inappropriate. How would U.C. suggest he approach this sense of 'freedom' therefore?

U.C: STAGES

'Growth occurs in stages; and if it is to be normal, natural, and healthy then it must be unforced. Life is growth, and for life to be harmonious there must be room to grow. You say you don't know quite what to do within the sessions, and I say back to you: use it for a time of growth. 'How?' I already hear you cry. Well, first of all remember that you both took the decision to emerge from the lulling serenity of the tapes, and place yourselves in a silent situation – a good move as far as we were concerned because it meant I had the opportunity to work through Ann. This was planned. Ann has work to do with me. 'Fine – jolly good for Ann, but where does that leave me?' you say. It appears to leave you rather out on a limb, left to your own devices.

'Now, I said you must feel free to do whatever you want during the sessions, and I meant just that. Referring back a moment to what I said about growth occurring in stages, then as far as the sessions are concerned you have reached a plateau. Freedom can be frightening, bewildering. This is a different way of communing for you than any you have ever been used to. You ask me what to do. First of all, I want to stress that if you wish to talk to me at any time during the sessions, then please do so. You will not interrupt me as I can switch from one thought to another quite smoothly – a little trick you will learn when you come here! Or else talk mentally to any of the group – ask who is here if necessary. Ann can let you know. Or read – yes, read if you feel that would help. An extra light would not bother any of us. Think about your book, about friendship, about beauty, about nature. Above all, let it be a companionable time for you. Don't feel restrained. Gradually you may find that freedom brings joy, and you can move gently from the plateau and grow into another stage. Freedom can give wings to growth. Remember, that although you appear to be sitting alone, you are very much a part of us.

'Good-night.'

24th SEPTEMBER, 1989 – Unknown Communicator

Before the session began, I asked U.C. several questions about what was happening to me at this time during my sleep life. Also a question about who to pray for each day since the list seemed to be growing somewhat! U.C. began to answer the questions about my sleep life, and had just finished the first paragraph when it was time for Jules to join us. After the prayer, Jules referred to U.C's last response, saying he could not have hoped for a better answer to what mental posture to adopt in the sessions. It even gave a scent of *relative* freedom. And he supposed that because he felt in such a mental prison these days, U.C's affirming that 'freedom can give wings to growth' seemed all the more alluring, yet still out of reach. If only the core belief behind what is sensed as a tense attitude could be found! However, he didn't expect to be spoon-fed, and guessed that U.C. was busy answering Ann's more important questions, so he'd leave it there and relax with whoever was present for the time being.

U.C. to Ann: WORKING WHILE ASLEEP

'First of all you ask why you have been waking at around 2 a.m. every night for the past week, with conversations ringing in your ears, hearing Lawrence's voice saying 'Yes' loudly, and feeling intensely hot with a band of heat particularly pronounced around your waist.

'To answer your questions one at a time. I mentioned to you a couple of sessions ago that I would be showing you how to work with suicides, drug addicts etc. We feel you are ready for this kind of work now – which means moving among very disturbed people both incarnate and discarnate – and it has begun in earnest during your sleep life. The best time for you to be with us is for a couple of hours or so, about *one* hour after you have fallen asleep. When we decide you have 'done enough' for one night you return closer to the body and, at the moment, enter it rather suddenly – thereby waking yourself up abruptly. (I was aware of U.C. thinking, although not dictating, that a couple of hours was sufficient also to enable me to experience 'ordinary' dreams, which we all need. A.H.). Two of the group always accompany you back to make sure of your safe return, and you partially remember conversations with them, and, in fact, heard Lawrence saying, 'Yes,' in reply to Duncan who was asking if you were all right. You feel very hot because of the alterations to your energy levels.

'Now I think the band of heat around your waist is caused by your own imagination trying to see yourself in protective clothing. I would be the last person to say this kind of work is easy, particularly as I know you have Parkinson's disease to cope with as well, but *you can do it*. I know you are not afraid; keep up your daily prayer work and get plenty of rest. It might be useful to have a glass of water to drink when you wake at night.

'Speaking of prayer work leads me to your next line of questioning. I know the list of people to pray for seems to be growing daily, bewildering you by its size. May I suggest you take a theme a day, i.e. children, the environment, friends, the sick, the bereaved, and so on. Obviously, if anything of urgent need crops up then this must take priority.

'Jules, welcome. I am glad you found my words helpful. Mental attitudes often seem to change when you have given up bothering with them. One day you will hear yourself saying: 'Oh, dash it – it looks as if I shall never alter,' and suddenly find that you have.

'Returning to you, Ann, for a moment. Energies are moving in you and I know this is giving you pains in your head. Try to imagine seeing the top of your head open to the sky; try to imagine looking through the top of your head – see blue skies, birds, clouds, soft rain, gentle sunshine. This may help towards the release of the energies, and the pain should be reduced.

'Good-night.'

27ᵗʰ SEPTEMBER, 1989 – Unknown Communicator
Jules said he didn't have a question because he felt too full of answers that he had not yet fulfilled in action; so he didn't know what to say. (He was also having difficulty in adjusting his stance to these new sessions, or even finding one in which he felt comfortable. His only stance therefore was to feel a bit dismal).

U.C: (to Ann) HAPPY DISCARNATE CHILDREN
'So you have already begun your work with suicides. You can be of particular help to Adrian because of your sympathetic, friendly link with his brother, whom you both wish to help. You felt unwell last weekend and experienced disturbed nights because the death had only just occurred and you were already 'on the scene'. It explains too your feeling

51

of depression over the weekend as you were caught up in the web of despair surrounding Adrian.

'I am glad you took as your theme, 'children', for the subject of prayer this evening. I, like many here, revel in visiting the children who are with us. They are delightfully tender and fresh, sparkling with joy. The homes they live in are so filled with love that no child ever fails to respond. Every grieving mother on earth would be so thrilled to see her child developing in such a warm cocoon that her tears would be wiped away.

'Good-night.'

1ˢᵗ OCTOBER, 1989 – Unknown Communicator
Heightened sentience, or perception, is sometimes a tender aspect of mediumship. Warmth floods over me – like having an electric fire switched on – whenever U.C. enters the room.

However, I have to admit that often after U.C's arrival, if my thoughts are having a tendency to wander, then they still do! U.C. 'sits' on my left side. It seems that he is sitting on the bed. He has a warm, compassionate presence, very soothing, I stare at the space – a funny experience because I know he is looking straight at me and can see me. Yet, at the same time, he feels as close to me as would a friend whom I could see in the physical. Sometimes he asks me to hold out my left hand, palm uppermost with the fingers stretched out straight. I can feel a cold sensation passing over my hand, above and below it. Other times what feels like a small rock, pebble or stone is pressed into the palm and I am told to close my fingers over it and hold it tightly.

As a general rule, U.C. and one or more of our Group arrive between 7.40 – 7.45 p.m. The word 'arrive' sounds rather official. Let me say rather that I 'know' they have come into the room. I am not sure even *how* I know this. I suppose it is similar to how I can sense that Gemma, our cat, has quietly entered. I don't have to see or hear her; I am just aware of the fact.

Taking down dictation for U.C. seems so easy to me. There I sit with pad and pen, and it's just as if I am listening to a radio broadcast and able to take down everything that is said at a steady pace. My hand and pen don't seem to belong to me, and yet another part of me knows that they do.

There are occasional pauses; sometimes I am taken back several sentences in order to make an alteration. But I *know* my own mind is not there. As soon as the dictation is over, I put down the notes aware that U.C. has gone. Then back come my thoughts – often picking them up exactly where I had left off.

Here now is the exchange between U.C. and Jules on this first day of October.

Jules recalled U.C's attention to a couple of months ago when U.C. had said that we make prisons out of our mistakes and human failings.

Regarding Jules' stance in the sessions he felt in just such a prison which, when examined with awareness, showed feelings of guilt and anxiety at not being able to appreciate, or reciprocate to those others invisibly present each time the companionable harmony he suspected was offered him.

U.C: FRIENDLY SILENCE

'You, Jules, seem to be tightening your bonds closer and closer around yourself, rather like an Egyptian mummy. But within this tight outer coating *you* are very much alive and warm. It is this warmth that stretches out to us in bewilderment for help because you want to feel relaxed, though the method escapes you. I can only reiterate that *nothing* is expected of you. As I have said, we welcome your presence, which does add support and protection for Ann. Now, once again I can suggest you use the time in whatever way you wish. One or other of the Group are always here – often to give a boost, a re-charge, to Ann's receiving channel. This is especially useful to me if Ann is tired or unwell for any reason. Often the Group just like to sit in quiet, companionable silence – they need refreshment from their duties just as you do. It is unlikely at the moment that any of the Group will communicate with you in the way I am doing. They were able to speak to you over a period of years, and gave valuable and unstinting service in helping to prepare Ann for this work.

'As I have said, they still like to join with you both, and you know how silence can be extremely friendly and consoling. If you come in feeling tense or frustrated, then these emotions are understood and accepted; after all, we have all experienced them. Self-acceptance of how *you* feel from moment to moment is what is important. Within the course of half an hour to forty minutes you will vary considerably in how you feel. You may come in tense and end up relaxed, and vice versa. So do not think you have to adopt any particular stance. Just be yourself. Experience yourself in the moment.

'Good-night.'

4th OCTOBER, 1989 – Unknown Communicator
Jules had found that U.C's picture of the situation somehow 'clicked' with him and had solved the problem. Now U.C. had spoken of 'Love', perhaps the most important lesson, and he had spoken of 'Freedom' in a rather intriguing way. But, unlike so many pundits/teachers either here or discarnate, he had not so far mentioned the practice of meditation – somewhat refreshingly! Was this omission significant?

U.C:
'Well, I was talking inwardly to Ann just now about freedom, so it is interesting, Jules, that you should continue the theme.

'Freedom comes before meditation. It is impossible, I may say, to practice true meditation until true freedom has been won, been gained. Far too much emphasis is placed on the art of meditation with sometimes disastrous results. People sit in circles, sit alone, trying to meditate and finding it well nigh beyond them to achieve! The small mind keeps interrupting. So, first of all, one needs to find a way to break free from the personality – to be aware of it, to function in it, but at the same time to realise how much it can make you play games with yourself. So here I am back again stressing discipline, which seems contradictory when I have headed this dictation freedom! I know I have spoken to you before – probably at

55

length – about discipline and self awareness: checking thoughts as they arise and so forth. Once you begin to do this, you are winning your spurs towards freedom. And once some sense of freedom from the bonds of the personality is felt, a sense of the Real You being in command, so that you are not at the personality's beck and call, then and *ONLY THEN* can meditation be attempted. Much has been written on the subject, on the different methods to adopt, but my method is oh so simple!

'You obviously choose a quiet room, and a quiet time of the day. You wear very loose, comfortable clothing. You sit in a comfortable chair, take some deep breaths – no special exercises to be used – just normal breathing but deeper than usual, and then let go. I used to imagine myself in a warm, soapy bath, every muscle relaxed in the warm water.

With eyes closed, give yourself up to this delightful sensation, and let colors★ and shapes swirl behind closed eyelids. To begin with these shapes will swing around rather haphazardly. But gradually your 'personal shape' will emerge – and it *is* different for each person, just as snowflakes are different. This is what you then center★ the mind upon; but very gently, unforced. The time will then come when your 'personal shape' shows itself as soon as you sit down. This is the *heart* of your Inner Being, infinitely precious, and with the help of this gently beating heart, your true mind will open and receive blessing. *This* is meditation.

'Good-night.'

★U.C's spelling, not mine

8th OCTOBER, 1989 – Unknown Communicator
Jules was impressed with U.C.'s view of meditation, saying
it was for him the most realistic yet encountered; one had to
'realise' how much the personality plays games with itself. But
did these 'games' mean the kind where we ascribe reasons for
our actions which are not the *real* reasons, or did he mean
another kind of game of which we are not yet aware?

U.C: PLAYING GAMES

'Now, in that particular instance I was referring to the
deceptions the personality employs continually in pretence.
The games played could be called 'Let's Pretend'. 'Let's
Pretend' we are not whom we suspect we *really* are. Let us
carry out an action while all the time deceiving ourselves as
to the *true* motive behind it. The personality frequently
distorts what the Higher Self wants for it. It may be quite a
simple, straightforward action that is required for the
personality to carry through, but the personality decides to
have a game with it: to enlarge it, to make a drama out of it,
to make it appear inconvenient at that time; even to lie about
it. So instead of the personality just quietly, easily, without
making any sort of fuss, getting on with what is required of
it, a valuable opportunity is lost to free itself from the snares
and traps it sets. The personality is a great actor; it loves being
center stage, dressed up for the role. Yet, if you can throw
away all these false trappings, these masks (which can happen
if self-awareness is regularly practised) and stop playing the
game of 'Let's Pretend', then you are on the way to freedom.

'Let's Pretend' is for children, but the Higher Self is adult, mature, and He seeks a mature vehicle through which to express Himself. It is not a game, it is not pretending to say that you are one of His counterparts. So, by allowing Him freedom of expression, you are freeing yourself from your games, and gently moving towards a time when you will be ready for meditation. The majority of people cannot meditate because they are trapped in a childish personality, and you would not expect a child to be capable of meditation! *And yet I say to you that almost all children* are, in fact, closer to a natural, freer form of meditation than most adults.

'Goodnight.'

11ᵗʰ OCTOBER, 1989 – Unknown Communicator
Jules could see that the kind of game U.C. was talking about referred to something soberingly deeper than had been thought, and this now caused him to review his early attempts with still greater suspicion. More immediately though, there flashed into his mind sudden consciousness of a tension-causing belief he had held during the recent years of trance sessions and most particularly in these sessions with U.C. It was: 'I *have* to grow spiritually. I *have* to aspire. Otherwise I am not worthy of all this discarnate attention.' On the contrary, however, Rajneesh had once said 'Growth takes care of itself. It comes of its own accord; it is not that you have to grow. Accept whatsoever you are and growth follows.' Jules wondered if discovery of this sort of false belief of his was perhaps a small step to realising the deeper game that U.C. meant. 'Sorry if this sounds a bit muddled,' he said.

U.C: LOVE AS ESSENTIAL TO HUMAN GROWTH

'Not muddled at all! Yes, yes, yes, you have hit the nail on the head. Your anxiety about growth has indeed been one of the games your personality has been playing.

'But at last you have acknowledged it out loud, and in so doing have loosened one of the bonds I was talking about two dictations ago: the bonds that hold you like an Egyptian mummy. You had persuaded yourself, convinced yourself I think, that you were not worthy to 'meet' us face to face because you felt you had not grown. As you rightly say, this particular belief *was* stunting your growth. But *you* had to acknowledge this to yourself. You disliked yourself and were not allowing love to flow naturally, yet love is as essential to human growth as water and nutrients are for the growth of plants. The Group had often spoken to you in the past, I have been told, about how one has to learn to love oneself before one can begin to love another. Love is acceptance – a favourite theme of mine I know, but I make no excuses for it. In accepting oneself as one is, without pretence, without playing 'Let's Pretend', but beginning to love oneself – a healthy, warm love, not narcissistic in any way – then one can begin to accept another's shortcomings and still love them too. It is, of course, a well-known fact that we dislike the faults in others that are most apparent in ourselves. If, however, we love these faults in ourselves, then it follows naturally that we love them in another. Then indeed we begin to 'Love Thy Neighbor as Thyself'.

'But I digress. Ann felt I was being more serious than usual last dictation, and she was right. The personality's habit of playing games and not listening with the best of its ability to the inner voice of the Higher Self can have repercussions. It is sad to witness precious incarnations slipping by. Intensive thought and planning has taken place beforehand to enable the personality to be in the right place at the right time for advancement. However, wastage never really takes place for long – after all, human beings are not throwaway objects and people often learn valuable lessons without realising it. You have done well, Jules, to see a truth. Once growth begins, the life force will keep it at the correct pace.

'Good-night.'

15ᵗʰ OCTOBER, 1989 – Unknown Communicator
Jules felt a sense of relief and gratification at U.C's answer last time. Perhaps now his feelings would begin to flow more naturally.

Yet in having to decide quickly this week on 'putting down' one of our cats because she seemed in distress and fouled the sofa, he was surprised at his own lack of emotion over the matter. Ann was overcome by the act, even tearful, while he felt a distinctly cold fish – despite having been very fond of the animal. Also, could U.C. comment on the rightness or otherwise of putting animals down, or putting them out of the physical? Is it for us to judge, and to act in this heavy way?

U.C: BEING TRUE TO ONESELF
'Now, your second question first. Do humans, or should humans, take the responsibility to have an animal or bird

humanely removed from its physical body? To this I say yes, but with a proviso: *that the animal should be seeming to request it in its own way.* It *knows* instinctively when its time on earth has come to an end. It will make the need known to whoever has it in his/her care. The need will show itself by ill health for example, by personality disorders, or by what you would describe as anti-social behaviour. Your cat would have died, indeed was ready to die, two months ago.* But a chance came for its development and it was guided to you. The love you both extended to this cat gave it security, a chance to express love and affection in return, and also a chance to build up a weakened physical body. But the cat *was* ailing, and its body would not have continued to live much longer. It had suffered in this incarnation, and therefore it reacted to a certain drama in a way that made you both decide to take quick, instant action. Animals often do this, but humans – through over-sentimentality – hang on to their pets by artificial means long past the time when they should have discarded the body. (Pause). I have been told that your cat's name is Peggy, and that she is being well cared for. When she returns again to earth, she will be much stronger.

'To turn to your first statement. Ann's heart center is almost completely open now, but her emotions are hard to bring under control. In other words, she hasn't learnt to feel and yet be at the same time detached. You on the other hand have, I agree, a more closed heart center. To be fair to you however you are used to living in the mind.

---

* Peggy was a stray who we had taken in two months ago.

Your mind could see the practicality of the solution you had both arrived at, and at the same time you knew that it would be false to express a sentimentality you did not honestly feel. You were each being true to yourselves in your different ways; you each have very different personalities. You have both been observing your reactions and this too is healthy. You are not plodding from one moment to another like robots. Ann felt emotion – good. You felt no emotion – also good. You were both being true. It is not so much what you express that matters, but what you observe yourself either feeling or not feeling. From this comes a clearer picture of *who you are*, and that is what is important.

'Good-night.'

SELF AWARENESS

18th OCTOBER, 1989 – Unknown Communicator

Autumn was colouring the trees around the house; hot summer days were just a memory. My bedroom curtains were drawn to before each session, and instead of gazing at blue skies, my eyes were now closed. This evening seemed no different at first when our friends arrived, bringing with them peace and tranquillity. But then my thoughts came into sharp concentration; I caught my breath as I seemed 'lifted' out of my everyday self. A shutter in my mind snapped open and I saw standing in front of me a pair of black feet thrust into open, thonged sandals, the legs clad in faded blue jeans, frayed at the ankles. From there upwards the vision dissolved into a brightness that eclipsed all else. I was aware of being in the presence of someone to whom no problem was too small to help solve. The love that radiated from him sprang from a well of understanding and compassion such as I have never before encountered. I knew it was the Unknown Communicator.

His work at the moment I felt to be particularly focussed around the development of human beings on earth. He quietly told me he was glad I was going to try to have his dictations published.

Jules entered at this point and said that we were both thankful for U.C's clear statement on the position regarding our cat, Peggy.

And he felt clearer than he had ever been on the practical effects of self-awareness as a main rudder on the spiritual path, the 'Way of the Pilgrim'.

Tonight's question was about self-awareness compared to what is commonly known as 'self-consciousness' – a weak and negative condition. How does anyone begin to overcome this latter state, which causes such anxiety and tension?

U.C: SELF-CONSCIOUSNESS AND SELF-AWARENESS

'A babe is born. He/she enters into the physical world, bringing with him the make-up for the personality of this new incarnation. To use an analogy: the personality can be likened to a clown who arrives at the dressing room before the performance with his bag of props, which he applies to himself as he has been taught in order to practice his craft. So it is with the emerging infant – he arrives with his bag of props. These props will contain all he needs for earth this time round, mixed in with 'leftovers' from previous lives. Like the clown, he dons his mask – his persona. Unlike the clown, however, his performance will most likely last for many years!

'So to recap: here we have the new personality with a purpose to fulfil in life, surrounded by others who also have reasons for being on earth. The child begins to grow, but because of external circumstances may feel insecure. He may have an uncomfortable feeling that his face just doesn't seem to fit; that somehow he is in the wrong place at the wrong time – metaphysically impossible of course as the family is selected beforehand. The poor perplexed child does not recall this fact, so he feels his bag of props has something vital missing. What it is he doesn't know, but he begins to feel more and more conscious that this is the case. Self-consciousness therefore begins to become acute, and *it is a hindrance* because it means that attention is wrongly focussed towards one's own personality. You find yourself watching yourself all the time, or more painfully feeling that others are! For a sensitive person this can be hell.

'The practice, the persistent practice, of self-awareness however can really help with this problem – and I don't think problem is too strong a word – for it shifts the center of attention away from the personality and moves it inwards. With the attention shifted off the personality you can develop self-forgetfulness, and the personality can begin to relax, to loosen tension, as it feels that all eyes are not on it.

'The personality is a puppet, and will respond to the strings being pulled by the puppet master, the Higher Self. Indeed, it longs for this because its self-consciousness is caused by loneliness of spirit. Self-awareness helps to link it to its source, and it no longer feels lost in a crowd of other lonely people.

'Good-night.'

22ⁿᵈ OCTOBER, 1989 – Unknown Communicator
Jules remarked that U.C. obviously understood self-consciousness very well. He also hoped for reassurance that nothing vital was in fact missing from his 'bag of props'!

Anyway, self-awareness seemed, as ever, a major key. It bothered him, though, that he might not be practising this properly because, while he realised he had only just restarted, he still could not find the truth behind his own irritations and criticisms in the sense that we 'dislike the faults in others that are most apparent in ourselves' – recently mentioned by U.C. Irritation, even rising sometimes to anger, at junk mail through the letterbox for example seemed quite unconnected with, or opposite to one's own behaviour faults – as did most other instances. Maybe he wasn't probing deep enough, or in the right way. Could U.C. give some specific guidance on the technique perhaps?

U.C: UNCOVERING THE TRUE SELF

'First of all, I want to give you absolute reassurance that there is nothing missing from your 'bag of props'. Rest easy on this one.

'You worry that you are not practising self-awareness properly, but you are, as you say, at the beginning of this exercise. I do not argue with this statement of yours, although at such an early stage I rather think you are being too hard on yourself. The true self has been covered for years by layer upon layer of outer coverings and these have to come off one at a time.

Each day you go through the same motions of getting up, getting dressed etc. etc; probably you do all this without even thinking about it, or maybe it seems a chore. Indeed, some days everything may seem tedious. You react to people in the same set way and so on. Try standing a little aside of yourself one morning. Watch your face in the mirror perhaps looking tense, and then try moving slowly, deliberately, concentrating on what you are doing, with very relaxed movements. I realise you will not be able to keep this up for any length of time, but for a moment or two you will get a glimpse of how your Higher Self moves. Try to watch yourself, too, in how you react to other people. For example, if you have begun a conversation and hear yourself once again responding in the old familiar pattern that you have become so heartily sick of, then try to be aware of this and alter the pattern of speech right there and then. These simple practices will assist in loosening the covers.

'Remember receiving a parcel as a child? You couldn't wait to get the wrappings off, and once one corner had been torn away enabling you to see what was inside, it made you all the more eager to expose the whole gift. So it will be for you, once you have begun to see your true self under the coverings. You know he is there, and the more self-awareness is practised the easier it will be to sense his presence. Even as I dictate this, I know I make it seem simple while knowing only too well that it isn't, but I felt I must try to give you some guidelines to follow. I trust they might be of some help.

'Now to the question of junk mail! I'm afraid I don't know what fault in you sends it to your door. I rather suspect that the fault lies with the attitude of society in general. However, you can be self-aware to observe what reactions it brings out in you and how you deal with them! The so-called consumer society will soon be consumed itself, and replaced by a more thoughtful, reflective one.

'Good-night.'

25ᵗʰ OCTOBER, 1989 – Unknown Communicator
Jules thanked U.C. for the reassurance, and said that not only did the techniques suggested seem practicable but also very suited to his mood at the moment.

He felt psychologically as though he were in a paper bag, trying to burst out of it while not knowing quite what was out there. Then he had thought: 'Wait a minute. If I grow spiritually, will this growth begin to diminish all those aspects of life I now enjoy?' Perhaps though, it was more a matter of 'the light' infiltrating even these, enhancing one's appreciation of them, regardless of their stature. 'Now is that right, or not?' he asked.

U.C:

'Absolutely quite right. You cannot lose what you have rightfully earned, rightfully inherited. You were born a child of God – pure, free. Living on earth, struggling with existence, curtails that freedom, sullies that purity. A child of God is born in grace, but lives at times an ungraceful, top-heavy life. After many trials and unhappiness, you have now found yourself in a balanced, secure environment. But a small voice nags at you: 'Can this all be as suddenly snatched away from me as it suddenly came?' Don't be afraid. The new emerging you, the one that longs to change, can only add a new dimension to what you already have. Once the tension is lifted from you, the fear melted away, I think you will be amazed at how even lovelier the world you inhabit will appear. Outer changes in your life have taken place and *will* remain secure. Inner changes will flood them with the colors

68

of that inner world where the true you resides. We, who know you and love you, realise that your personality needs a secure earth base. This, as I have said, you now have. To quote a phrase you know well: 'Nothing can harm you, nothing can really hurt you'.

'So when you feel ready, gradually begin to ease yourself out of one of your coverings. You will feel lighter, freer, less weighed down. You will not be moving into uncharted seas because your Higher Self has always been there. He knows the way.

'As I have said to you before – don't be surprised by rebuffs if you make overtures of help and friendship. Most people are locked away inside themselves, playing out their own psychological dramas, seeming in isolation very lonely, while their guides stand faithfully by trying to help in every way they can.

'Rejoice, my friend, that you are beginning to find the key to happiness. Don't let anxieties hold you back. Step forward in faith. The season of autumn on earth is often used symbolically for a clearing away of old, wasted foliage. It just drops to the ground to be absorbed, to replenish the earth for new growth in the spring.

'Good-night.'

Prior to the start of this session I asked U.C. why I was feeling so unwell this particular day. The Parkinson's disease was very bad with shaking down the right hand side of my body, difficulty with speech and walking. Here is his answer to me:

'You are being almost ultra sensitive to what you see as

the needs of others. Try to keep this in perspective; it is impossible for you to help everyone. Those you seek to help have their chosen paths to tread. Surround them with healing, loving thoughts of course, but do not worry about them. Let them walk their individual paths and you walk yours. If you were out walking in the physical world you would not expect to hold the hands of all your companions. So it is with the Way. Each *must* find their own piece of track. You carry on your shoulders the burden of Parkinson's borne for two weaker members of your group, thereby freeing them for their development. Don't try to take any more burdens on at the moment. Enjoy your life, your prayer work. Yes, sing out loud for joy if you want to. Why not!'

29th OCTOBER, 1989 – Unknown Communicator
Jules was glad of what U.C. had said last time. It was only his own emotional reaction he found disappointing. He remembered one metaphysical writer (Clarice Toyne) who speculated that people generally did not accept this knowledge because it seemed 'too good to be true'. He had thought her theory feasible, and felt slight impatience with them. Now, however, attempting self-awareness of his own reaction to this personal material it seemed he was coming across the same block in himself: 'too good to be true'. Headwise he knew it was true; heart-wise he was not rejoicing, perhaps not quite believing it of himself.

How could he ever begin, therefore, to 'ease out of one of the coverings'? Use the head for the time being?

U.C. took several minutes to begin his answer. I felt him trying various approaches before commencing; (it is odd to have such acute awareness of another's mind at work, detachedly knowing it is not yours). U.C. knew that Jules had a good deal of background knowledge of the metaphysical field, and he didn't wish to keep repeating himself. At the same time he wished to supply enough information for any other reader faced with the same dilemmas as Jules. This he found difficult to do in a concise manner as there was a great deal he could have said.

U.C:

'Yes, that is a good starting point and you have to begin from somewhere. Why does goodness seem too good to be true? I think earth has conditioned you to think otherwise; not just you of course but countless others. Conditions on earth, events and feelings that you have experienced, combine to make you appear a very long way from that child of God, pure and free, that I mentioned in the last dictation. But these simple, loving words are the truth. I just think that perhaps feelings of unworthiness, however misplaced, make you reluctant to take that step of faith. It seems difficult for the adult to become pure and free, but that really is not the case.

'Remember we were talking about the 'bag of props' just recently, and I said you had nothing missing? Well, that 'bag of props' contains all the ingredients for your freedom. I feel that you are an earnest seeker after truth and freedom – indeed, if you were not, I would not have used these phrases to you because they are powerful statements. A struggle is going on in you, as if you were being pulled both ways, and (here I may be wrong) I think you feel that if you fully accept the complete meaning of these words you would be called upon to make a commitment you suspect you are not quite ready for. If this is the case, don't worry about it. Think on the words when you are quiet and alone. Give yourself time to assimilate them.

'I think you will be able to sink into the absolute feeling of security, the sense of peace, that they can give to one.

'Yes, this is what they have achieved for me over the years – years of struggle with myself. Now I experience that steady flow of love continually pouring forth from the Source. There are some ripples in the flow, but always I feel it there, this love, directed towards me – a child of God. I, in turn, as part of my role, can pass that love to all on earth – each and every one of you who are all born children of God.

'Good-night.'

THE POWER OF LOVE

1ˢᵗ NOVEMBER 1989 – Unknown Communicator

U.C. was present almost as soon as I sat down, not long after 7 p.m. There was a powerful flow of energy in the room and it seemed as if many people were present.

U.C. dictated the following:

'Child, we will soon be coming to the end of this particular pilgrimage together for a while, to give you time to start putting the dictations into book form. I will dictate to you both still, but these may be kept aside for the time being. I will indicate clearly soon when the dictations for publication will be stopping. You have both served me well.'

After a pause of seven to eight seconds, with my hand resting very lightly on the paper, the pen began to move slowly over the paper and a signature was formed, revealing an identity which he preferred we keep to ourselves.

Another pause followed – this time about one minute in duration – and then energy really seemed to be pumping in U.C's veins as he began to dictate again.

'It is hot in the fields and the Negroes have to work hard; long, toiling days for very little reward. Everyman is born equal in the sight of God. Why should the color of your skin make you any less equal? Many die and the time for mourning them is short. Conditions *must* be improved; good housing and sanitation should be the right of everyone, black and white.

'Slavery was abolished in this country a long time ago. Abolished in the statute books, but not in men's hearts and *that* is where it matters. But the black man is a free man if he fulfils his purpose to God. He is only answerable to God and no one can take away his thoughts. Until all men love one another as brothers there can be no equality, whatever lip service is paid to that word. Not only in America are men held in slavery, but in countries all over the so-called free world; held in prison for speaking the truth, for loving God who gave them breath. So love one another, work for freedom – but there must be no violence of any kind. Dignity, clear thinking – these qualities will win the day.'

There was tremendous force and vehemence behind these words of U.C's and the pen flew over the paper with amazing speed. My hand could hardly keep up with the flow of the dictation. I don't know whether or not he meant it for the book, but place it on record nevertheless.

When Jules came in, he referred to the previous session, thanking U.C. for a very thought-provoking answer, particularly the last bit. He valued this direct experience above all, concerned to know what it was like from someone presumably closer to the Source than he was. He now had two questions: the first was about U.C's theory that Jules was afraid of a commitment he felt not quite ready to make.

Underneath, did U.C. mean perhaps that the idea of any commitment was false, or misleading? For it occurred to Jules that whatever his own true feelings really were, actual acceptance in the heart that one was a 'child of God' would not conceivably feel like a commitment as much as a joy, a peace, a power even. The word commitment sounded comparatively like a marriage licence! He would contemplate as suggested, however.

The second question was whether our *experience of good intent* within us here on earth was that same love only very much diluted by the time it reaches and manages to penetrate someone like Jules on earth, if it does at all. The good intent, for example when, quite alone, we might rescue an insect, save the life of a bird, animal, or tree. Is this a very diluted, scaled down version of 'that steady flow of love continually pouring from the Source'?

If so, here would be the 'religion' within everyone in a way most evident to us, surely?

U.C.

'I am inclined to use somewhat evangelical-sounding language at times, I'm afraid. Yes, commitment brings freedom to feel joy, peace. I wondered, after I used the word, if maybe you might read into it the reverse of these emotions. It sounds a stern word in the way I used it in reference to yourself. But you are quite right to feel that acceptance of being a child of God in your heart brings release from the worries and tensions of the world. I think perhaps I meant commitment to imply that, once you have experienced joy in the fullest sense, there can be no substitute. Nothing on earth literally can fulfill one in quite the same way.

'To turn now to the question about love. You ask: Is it a diluted form by the time it reaches someone like yourself? To this I reply: 'No.' Love cannot be diluted because love is All That Is, and All That Is lies present in its full power and majesty in everything. It is, as you say, in your feelings toward all life; insects, bird, etc. Your mind thinks that by the time it reaches you it must have come so far down through so many levels that you cannot experience it in the way I described. Your Higher Self *is* this love, and, as has been said to you before I know, He is closer to you than breathing. You are enveloped, surrounded, cocooned by this sweet flow of love from the Source in just the same way as myself. To use an analogy: it is like a river. It wants to be constantly moving. It doesn't want to be dammed back. So if you in turn pass it on to animals, birds, plants etc., it will keep it ever flowing free.

'Good-night.'

5ᵗʰ NOVEMBER, 1989 – Unknown Communicator
Jules said that U.C's use of the word 'commitment' was now crystal clear. But where the experience of love was concerned he felt himself a slow learner. Did U.C. mean that when he (Jules) experienced some sense of caring, of wanting to contribute something of value to the world, to fill in what he sees as lack, to share, to create beauty, to 'help' people etc… that the Higher Self's 'love' is the root of these feelings too? Are *these* a degree of the love, or are they purely psychological compensation and quite unconnected? Now, having said that,

Jules saw U.C's sentence: 'It all gets dammed up.' So do we just dam it up through fear all the time, rather than dilute it, as such?

U.C: LOVE CAN PERFORM MIRACLES

'Yes, the love in the way you describe it is the love as experienced by your Higher Self. Love cannot be altered, cannot be made different. Love is love upon whatever level it is being practised, however hesitantly to begin with.

'Whatever kindly act you do, whatever kindly thought you think, that is the selfsame love of which I was speaking.

'It is most important not to dam it up or dam it back. Let it flow with free expression. This may seem strange and slightly stilted to you, maybe even false to begin with – it may not seem natural to you. But the more you exercise it, letting it flow through you and out toward others, the more the power of love will be felt. It really can perform miracles and the most amazing miracle will start within your own personality, your own heart. You will find yourself really liking people and being liked back in return.

'This power of love is needed badly, oh so badly, in the world today – so much can be achieved through its application. Love helps to build bridges of faith, to cross barriers of race and creed. If man can really begin to experience love through all his bodies, then wars will cease, countries will pull down custom barriers, prisoners of conscience will be set free, animals will have the same right as humans, children will be educated for their place in the world instead of for academic achievement. The very young and the very old will have a dignified place within the family of man. It sounds like Utopia, I know. It *can* and *will* come about. The evolution of mankind will undam the false walls. True love is the highest and noblest of all the emotions and cannot be denied.

'Good-night.'

[This was dictated two days before the Berlin Wall began to be pulled down].

8ᵗʰ NOVEMBER, 1989 – Unknown Communicator

Jules did not have an exact question this time. He just felt warmed by confirmation of one's basic drives to good intent being a conscious link with one's Source, and underlined U.C's statement beginning 'Whatever kindly act you do…' So underneath the vanity and silliness of behaviour on the surface, dismaying as these were to witness in himself, he could also bear witness to his deeper sense of care about truth, love and beauty, which perhaps was his Higher Self trying to break through; a most encouraging revelation which brought It or Him into conscious earth life – as close as breathing. Yet this would take time to fully assimilate into practical behaviour, he felt. There was so much to 'unlearn', undo from himself as it were, and habits were so thickly encrusted that much of real value still seemed a long way off.

U.C:

'The Higher Self is your greatest, truest friend, Jules. The experience of beginning to know Him, to be aware of His gentleness, His patience, is a sincerely humbling one for most people. Just the knowledge that He is there, sharing every experience, has helped so many through dark and terrible times in their lives. His has been the hand they have clung to; His has been the hand that has wiped away their tears. As you rightly say, to begin to be aware that He is indeed closer to you than breathing is a revelation, a fact that has to slowly creep up on one, a fact that makes you almost hold your breath! You are his skin, his bones, his eyes and ears in the world of physical matter; the relationship is of the most intimate.

'But you are quite right to say that self-awareness should be approached gently. To suddenly undo several of the coverings I have mentioned would be too abrupt. It could make you feel rather naked. I am glad to hear you witness your feelings of good intent. To explore and concentrate on these will exercise them, will encourage you to bring them to the fore, helping you to cope with the 'sillinesses' of daily living. As you become even more aware of the presence of your Higher Self, these irritations will have less and less significance in your life.

'Good-night.'

12th NOVEMBER, 1989 – Unknown Communicator
U.C. arrived about 7.30 p.m. I had been praying about the recent events which had been taking place over the past three days in Berlin. U.C. dictated the following as far as 'The time is coming'. Then Jules joined us and U.C. drew his usual line a short way below his existing dictation, answered Jules' question and then finished dictating his original piece. Anyway here is his first dictation.

U.C:

'Child, the time is not far away now when the world of men will be unified to such a degree that a short time ago seemed impossible. A miracle is happening in your world – yes, miracle is not too strong a word. The time is coming. More and more in your world are being prepared to help. Strong, healthy, clear personalities are incarnating: personalities who do not have many problems of their own to overcome and are ready to serve the Hierarchy.'

When Jules came in he referred back to the previous session, saying that the emotional part of him would want to read U.C's first paragraph again and again to remind himself. But who *were* these 'people', these 'so many' who had become aware of the Higher Self? He realised of course that one did not necessarily need metaphysical study to achieve this, although the implication seemed to be that here was Jules with head-knowledge and years of discarnate contact, struggling for awareness while a mysterious proportion of others, somewhere, had attained without such advantages. It made him feel a bit backward. Were his concepts blocking him, and if so, which must he drop?

U.C.   THE COMPASSION OF THE HIGHER SELF

'Let me try to clarify for you, Jules. No, your knowledge, your intellectual understanding, is not getting in the way. It is a rare gift you have. I was quite simply referring to everyone, 'Everyman' if you like to call him that, the Christian of John Bunyan's 'Pilgrim's Progress'.

I say 'Everyman' because all who cry in the darkness of despair, who are suffering in mind and body, who have minds clouded by drink and drugs, who are mentally or physically handicapped – all these are helped, albeit in most cases unknowingly, by their Higher Selves. The Higher Self has so much compassion for the personality He has sent forth that He never abandons it like a rudderless ship. Although troubles at times seen ready to swamp one, to envelop one like a tidal wave, you can never go under. I said earlier that you have a rare gift and I meant every word I said. Few have the metaphysical insight you have acquired. I would not be able to dictate these scripts to you in the way I do if you did not have this knowledge, because few would appreciate what is happening between us – this link of communication with Ann in the middle frantically scribbling away, her hand trying to keep up with my thoughts.

'I suspect you feel very much alone at the moment, but what I dictated last time is also very, very true; namely Jules, that your Higher Self is closer to you than breathing. He is very aware of your perplexities and puzzlement. You are finding it difficult to contact Him. Am I right in thinking this? And you think that the knowledge you have is almost getting in the way, getting between you and the one you earnestly seek. But at least you know something about the One you look for. 'Everyman', as I call him, cries out to a nameless God, or rejects any thought of God at all. The point I wanted to make was that no one is ever turned away. No one is ever considered unworthy however low they may appear to have sunk in the eyes of their fellow man. However, in most cases they do not know this. Their aloneness is almost more than they can bear. They do not know that the hand they hold out is held; that the tears they shed are wiped away. Now this is where a book like *Between Heaven & Charing Cross* can help to light a candle in men's minds and hearts; help them to see that we, who no longer have a physical body, work to alleviate suffering. I agree with you that orthodox churchiness is often of little help. I hope I have helped you a little tonight.

'Good-night.'

15th NOVEMBER, 1989 – Unknown Communicator
Jules was glad of the explanation, which certainly had helped, and wanted to make sure he understood it. Those people then who experience the Higher Self's qualities of gentleness and patience touching them, do not actually know the source of the experience – attributing it, perhaps, to Jesus or Mohammed or some other religious figure, if anyone at all. Moreover it is only felt by those in desperate straits who reach out for help. News that the Higher Self is aware of perplexities and puzzlement was a relaxer on these in itself. Jules did indeed find difficulty in contact. But if concepts weren't getting in the way, he supposed that either his Higher Self had nothing to say to him or he was not in desperate straits, or he was not yet ready for practical co-operation because of his still enjoying his 'sins', figuratively speaking. Was he right?

U.C.
'I think you are slightly off beam, Jules, when you have an idea that your Higher self has nothing to say to you. He is

in contact with you all the time, giving words of encouragement – a helping hand here, a guiding thought there. You may not be consciously aware of this, and from how you phrase your statement I don't think you are; but I think you will agree with me when I say you have been trying hard to alter old habits, to 'get out of that rut' so to speak. You have made great efforts on your part to discover the new emerging you, and your Higher Self has been assisting. The Higher self is experienced in many different ways by different people, according to whether they are what I call heart or head people.

'The heart folk feel the gentleness, the patience of their Higher selves, while they are swamped by the surging swell of a great crisis, or simply bobbing in calm, still waters where they can be reflective and at peace with themselves.

'You, as we know, are a head person, but you are still on the receiving end of His gentleness and patience. His awareness of your 'perplexities and puzzlement' about your behaviour and thoughts is evidence of this. He has great compassion for you in your earnest desire to change and is ever looking for ways to helpfully influence you. You see, when the great cross-roads is reached in the life of an evolving personality and the decision to take the right Path is taken, this is a marvellous moment for the Higher Self, and you, my dear friend, have taken the right Path. The easier roads always appear enticing. They often appear straight, exciting amusements are spread out along the way; but the right road – ah, now that is a different matter. It looks tricky at first glance, difficult to see far ahead.

'Courage is needed to step onto that Path. To begin with it seems restrictive, there appear to be notices saying: 'Don't do things in the old way – try the new way'. Hard isn't it, to begin with? A lot to remember all at once! But as old habits drop away you feel lighter, fresher, it begins to make sense. You realise that you are not alone on this Path after all; kindly faces greet you wherever you look, the terrain becomes less stony, colors are brighter. Your Higher Self rejoices with you. Your hard work is at last rewarded.

'Good-night.'

UNDERSTANDING

19th NOVEMBER, 1989 – Unknown Communicator

I had been praying, before the session began, for a young girl, Caroline aged thirteen, whom I had seen on a recent television programme suffering from appalling burns, received while trying to rescue her young sister from a house fire. Tears came into my eyes as I recalled her face and arms and I thought of all her suffering. 'Do tears get in the way of prayer work?' I asked U.C. who arrived just before the prayer. He began by telling me privately how beneficial tears were in actual fact. Then he asked me to take down the following dictation:

'The human temple, within which the spirit dwells, is not destroyed. It cannot be destroyed if what happened was not caused by self-abuse. This young girl has lost what you call in earth terms 'her looks' but at the same time she also lost one of the tight outer coverings and her spirit can literally shine through. She would never have survived such terrible injuries if her spirit was not willing it. This one has a strong role to fulfill in life, and she is being prepared for it from a much earlier age than most.

'But don't be ashamed to cry for her. This is good. This

is how you feel. These tears of yours will flow over her as a gentle balm, a soothing ointment. Tears have healing properties when used with sincerity.'

Jules had been studying the previous session's answer and said he was sorry but it seemed as if U.C. was talking to someone else when saying things like the Higher Self was in contact with Jules 'all the time, giving words of encouragement – a helping hand here, a guiding thought there...looking for ways to helpfully influence' Jules. He certainly was not *consciously* aware of it. He had thought he might have been that morning in receipt of an idea to apologise to an old friend for thoughtless behaviour twenty-three years ago, but had come up against a very curious blank wall in trying to do so. *If* that meant it wasn't the Higher self's 'influence' – what was? Could U.C. give some examples of what he meant? Or could he at least be more specific please?

U.C: REBUFFS CAUSED BY EARTH INFLUENCES

'I know you feel unaware in your outer life of any kind of help from a higher source. You are quite right to say that I am not talking about the astral self but your Higher Self. I know too how you feel frustrated that everywhere, every way you turn seems blocked. But this is not because you lack any guidance from your Higher Self. It is because you are coming up against earth influences. You have fine inner ideas and thoughts that you wish to bring through into your daily life, but bang seems to go a door in your face. It hurts, puzzles, and baffles you.

'I cannot explain this morning's incident, to which you refer, as I know nothing of the circumstances. You tell me you wished very much to make restitution to an old friend whom you feel you treated thoughtlessly twenty-three years ago. Another blank wall rises up to block you apparently. You seem to be on your own again. I *can* say this to you: your sincere desire to set the record straight – even though you seem to be unable to do so in earth terms – this sincere desire *will* have made itself felt, even though you may not see any results. A good thought is a good thought – even if you cannot physically make it move mountains.

'This is an important point you have raised here tonight, Jules, because it is very easy, oh so very easy, for someone like me to sit here dictating in glowing terms about your progress and the help you receive from your Higher Self. It is a different matter to be sitting on earth feeling helpless.

'This feeling you experience applies of course to almost the whole of the human race. But I really don't know what else to say to help you. You don't want strings of platitudes and placebos; I would not wish to insult your intelligence by handing these out like candy to a baby. I can do no more than repeat what I have said before, namely that you are not alone. But, by golly, I need reminding of the fact that it is one of the hardest things to believe. Thank you for your frankness: this is a two-way communication and I need to know exactly how you feel and react. Too many teachers talk too loosely about love and its effects, forgetting what it was like to suffer the seeming absence of these effects in daily life. I, in turn, must be frank with you. Quite honestly, much more thought is needed by us here on this subject.

'Good-night.'

[While U.C. was dictating the latter half of this session, I was aware of a sadness pervading his thoughts because he felt he had somehow failed to make clear to Jules how to experience the closeness of the Higher Self in his everyday life].

22nd NOVEMBER, 1989 – Unknown Communicator

I had not asked U.C. a question, he simply asked me to write the following dictation:

U.C:

'It is beginning to happen. Men are even now beginning to understand one another. Language difficulties do not seem important because the universal language is the smile, the touch on the arm, the clasp of the hand, the look of sympathy and understanding that passes between people. Words are not needed. A human being is a human being regardless of where he lives.

Needs are the same: the need for companionship, for a secure base, and most of all for freedom and equality. Soon East and West will have no division. The term 'Eastern block countries' – an ugly phrase I think – will disappear from common usage. There will be countries with their own traditions and customs, but the dividing line will seem more like that between counties in your country. As this pressure – that has always been present because of the line between so called East and West – eases, the smaller countries now caught in the middle will feel much more relaxed.

'At the moment they feel – and here I speak of the Middle East, South America and Africa – like a nut being squeezed in a giant nut cracker. As they become more relaxed so they will react less violently.

'The influence of One who has now come close to planet Earth is making itself felt. All who have experienced what it is like to be in His presence say that it is impossible to feel any other emotion than that of Love. The world is waking up from a long sleep and starting to respond.

'Good-night.'

[Jules came in while U.C. was dictating and then received a private communication from U.C.].

26th NOVEMBER, 1989 – Unknown Communicator
This evening Jules did not have a question to ask of U.C. He just wished to thank him for the private communication dictated after the previous session. Jules said he was most grateful for the sentiments expressed, and also that he was becoming more self-aware. In particular he was aware for the first time of hidden threads of fear running through his normal thoughts.

U.C:

'Thank you for what you have just said, and I will always try to give any help I can to you both.

'The personality seems so cut off, so insular, so inadequate to deal with problems which daily confront and surround it.

'Everyone has different obstacles to surmount and overcome, and different ways of tackling even the same *kind* of problem. The majority of people want to be one of the herd, one of the gang; they want only to associate with others who look like themselves. White people have long considered themselves superior, mainly because of the word association in their mind to their color: white representing purity. To be brown or yellow or black – well, your face quite literally does not fit! You are viewed with suspicion, and in many cases with hatred. You are almost certainly considered inferior.

'To follow a minority faith or creed – this is also viewed with scepticism and intolerance. Therefore, if you happen to be let us say a black unemployed Jew, then the dice is heavily loaded against you. Until the personality begins to evolve, unfortunately fear plays a major role in its make-up. The personality develops and fear begins to recede; a more patient, enlightened attitude starts to show itself toward its fellows. But the personality does not like to have its comfortable existence threatened in any way, so if anything is thrown up to cause a ripple, out shoots the threads of fear you describe. 'What is this? I don't like these feelings, I feel insecure,' it grumbles to itself.

'However, the developing personality begins to link up, albeit gradually, with its greatest ally – its Higher Self. Once it becomes aware of the Higher Self's existence – maybe he does not refer to it as the Higher Self but as a being greater than himself, or whatever name he chooses to call it by – then a feeling of comfort creeps in. The personality may not feel his Higher Self in his daily life, but a dawning sure certainty that Someone is around gives him that feeling of security to enable him to explore other facets of himself, to take steps into the unknown. Of course, like a child to begin with, fear makes you want to cling to what you know; but once growth has started it will not stop.

'Good-night.'

29th NOVEMBER, 1989 – Unknown Communicator
About one and a half hours before we began preparing for the session, Jules and I were in our sitting room idly chatting. My relaxed mood suddenly and quite inexplicably altered. Tears kept welling up. I felt angry and upset, and very alone. The familiar outlines of objects in the room blurred and faded.

With startling clarity I was experiencing myself as a young baby. No, much more than that, I was a tiny infant about to emerge from the womb, being pushed violently from side to side. I wanted to leave the confining atmosphere. I liked the idea, but the person to whose body I was attached was holding me back. I was suffocating. This person was terribly frightened, and someone with none too gentle hands persisted in tugging me. 'Oh, do let go! I can do it for myself. I want to break free if you would only just leave me to get on with it,' I was inwardly protesting.

Then I was alone with my mother who seemed afraid of me; afraid to cuddle me. I was crying with frustration for what seemed like hours on end. I remembered an opportunity had been offered, and accepted by me, to take on a debilitating illness, an illness which would only affect my physical body.

I had the chance to help others and I was eager to get on with it. The experience lasted about ten minutes and then the room came back into focus.

We moved into our respective rooms prior to 8 o'clock. U.C. arrived immediately. I told him what had happened and how the incident had disturbed me.

U.C: PARENTS AND BABIES

'The baby is a stranger, to even the most loving of mothers. The baby is a stranger and we are wary of a stranger, an unknown entity, suddenly entering our lives. Life does not prepare one for this new helpless being confronting you. The parents probably feel a strong mixture of emotions according to their own emotional make-up: pride, uncertainty, reluctance, genuine warmth etc. But the responsibility of being presented with a new, innocent life generally overwhelms all other feelings. One has training for other jobs but not this one! Oh, you can go to all the baby-craft classes in the world but that is only to learn theory.

'Don't look back too harshly towards your own parents. You have remembered being left to cry for long periods on your own, but you were born at a time when bringing up a baby had to be done according to the book. Crying 'out of hours' so to speak, was not allowed and you were impatient to 'get on'. This impatience still characterises much of what you do. Now you are anxious to leap ahead.

'But to go back to babies. Todays' young mothers have learnt the importance of cuddling their little ones, of keeping them close to their own bodies. The so-called primitive tribes, i.e. the native American Indians, the Eskimos, the Africans, knew this from way back – no baby carriages for them! The baby was always held close to the mother's breast, this being its primary function, of course – not as an object of titillation for men. It could be argued that men find the roundness of women's breasts so appealing because a primal feeling of longing to cling to their mother is aroused.

'But I digress. You have had a very valuable lesson revealed to you this evening. Those who watch over you took the opportunity of your mind being relaxed to take you on a journey of discovery back to the moment of your birth. Now you can see many sides of your personality, which had been hidden from you before. You can also be reassured that your Parkinson's disease is only felt by the *personality*. It does not and cannot affect the fundamental You. How you cope with it does, but needless anxiety about it will only create tension. You have a deeply understanding friend in Jules. You have shared and cared through many lives; enmity has never existed between you.

'If you have absorbed tonight's revelations, then the Parkinson's should begin to be less troublesome. Follow your instincts more. Try to be more sure of yourself, child. You will need to take it easy for a day or two because you regressed tonight back to a point that it takes many people many hours of therapy to achieve. We felt you were balanced enough to cope and a good deal of trapped energy has been released. Keep warm as the shock has chilled you.

'God bless you.'

After the finish of this dictation U.C. then indicated that he wanted to give the following heading:

HISTORICAL NOTES

'Babies, poor things, have been at the whim of passing fashion for generations.

'From the middle ages onwards in your country the wealthier classes felt it unfashionable to bring up their own babies, so the nurse and then the nanny was introduced. The wet nurse came to live in the household and therefore the mother did not even feed her own child. By the end of the last century the practice of wet nursing was beginning to be considered unhygienic – the wet nurses often liking a drop or two of drink. They were banished and the nanny arrived. Once the child was weaned it was relegated up to the nursery. Fashionable households vied with each other to employ the best nanny possible, and even a nursery maid or two. The child was by and large a stranger to its parents.

'Soon the first perambulators were being made and the poor baby was put into this unwieldy contraption to be pushed around the park. The advent of two world wars saw off the nanny, except in the most affluent of homes, and the pram began to disappear. At least the baby could lie flat in this and have the opportunity to explore its own fingers and toes, its own body – very important. Suddenly the pushchair appeared.

'This coincided with the building of high rise blocks of flats where space was at a premium. Pushchairs took up less space. The young child was expected to sit up in one of these, muffled in some kind of anorak suit so the poor thing could hardly move its arms around. This habit of being forced to sit in unnatural positions when young has led to many people having back problems in adult life.

'But at last the western world is beginning to see the all round practicality of carrying the infant in a sling; many fathers are carrying their baby in this way, and why not? The experience will help prepare them for a subsequent incarnation as a female and mother.'

Thoughts about babies and children still seemed to be in the forefront of U.C's mind, and after a pause of two or three minutes he composed the following poem entitled:

FOR A CHILD

You have eyes, ears and hands,
A heart of love to give your friends,
To parents, brother, sister, dog or cat,
If you give love, they'll give it back.
Like 'pass the parcel', around it goes,
Dropping its wraps,
Until it shows,
The secret present inside, aglow!

As U.C. finished the poem Jules came in for the session, fresh from contemplating the dictation on 'steps into the unknown'. Quietly, and with a smile on his face, he declared that under all the guidance received these months from U.C., and now as a result it seemed subtly from the inner source, (perhaps the very 'guiding thought' he had doubted), he might have come upon such a step – the means to be true to himself. Before, the axiom had appeared trite. Now at last a more practical intimation of it, a picture of 'The Way' had opened out: partly to do with relating and reacting to events from a deeper honesty 'within' him rather than from that which the surface self thought was expected of him by others. In practice this appeared to resolve anxiety if not fear on the spot. Did U.C. consider the intimation to be valid, and one moreover that could invite more influence from the Higher Self?

U.C: RELAXING WITH ONE'S TRUE FEELINGS

'Yes, Jules, I do agree very much with what you have just said. The more you can relax with what you sincerely sense are your true feelings, the nearer you will come to discovery, to finding your true self. After all, why be at the beck and call of other people? Why always react in a way you think they have come to expect of you? If others think they can get a response from you in a certain manner, they will often try to do so again and again. Like a child playing with a jack-in-the-box, the jack-in-the-box always jumps in the same fashion each time.

'Why not give people a surprise sometimes and act in a different way than they have come to expect? They may be taken aback, perhaps feel unsure of themselves and you, but they will come to respect you a good deal more. Or maybe there will be no reaction from them. That doesn't matter.

What *does* matter is the feeling of respect you have gained in yourself.

'To be true to yourself', is, I think, one of the most beautiful expressions in the English language. To extend that feeling further, you are beginning to be true to the source of your being. Once you have begun to absorb this feeling of being true, of knowing yourself, then you do not have to lean so heavily on other people for support. You are your own man – creative, responsive to the needs of the animal kingdom, aware of beauty, of natural beauty, of natural gaiety, of natural warmth.

'Now, Jules, tonight's dictations are the last ones for this book but I will still be with you each session so do talk to me. As a medium Ann is well in alignment with me now, and free flow of exchange can easily take place. I shall watch with interest the progress of our work.

'Good-night.'

At first satisfied with U.C's completion of his little book, we both privately began to feel that perhaps it was too short. Our opinion was confirmed by Paul Beard, a respected reviewer in the field, who had read the book up to this point. He suggested that it might be better to end at a 'more decisive stage of integrated action' on Jules' part. Meanwhile, as U.C. promised, the sessions had continued, and, looking at them, we saw something like such a stage further on.

Why then had U.C. ended so soon? It crossed our minds that he foresaw signs of 'bolshiness' on my part against continuing the mediumship and therefore decided to round his message off while the going was good! We do not know. By the time the decisive stage was reached, he had already indicated to me, when asked off the record, that he was content to leave the matter in our hands, so we have made these continuing dictations PART II.

While reading through the typescript, U.C's use of capitals began to cause us some concern. We knew that he was not being ostentatious, but recognised that others might not necessarily share the sense felt from him. It is a sense which tries to distinguish between a lower meaning and a higher one, between what is commonly experienced and what still awaits unfoldment or realisation in most human beings. Hence, the 'love' which perhaps in its lowest sense is 'desire' and in a closer sense is strong affection, falls as yet way below totally unconditional 'Love'; and the 'radiance' of a lamp is far short of the Love-filled quality of 'Radiance' from our Source. However, that said, we still felt that there was a too liberal sprinkling of capitals throughout the scripts. Therefore, we discreetly altered them with the occasional exception.

PART II

ALLOWING THE BLUEPRINT

LOVE AND FORGIVENESS

3ʳᵈ DECEMBER, 1989 – Unknown Communicator
Jules was late for this session and U.C. told me that he was
asleep – which in fact he was! He came in eventually and, after
the prayer, apologised. He then took his first opportunity,
since U.C. had completed the initial section of the book, to
compliment our tutor on the valued help these dictations had
given us both. Jules now wanted to ask if this relaxing into
the truth of himself was perhaps the lowest rung of a U.C.-
type state of 'relaxing into Truth' with a capital 'T' – so that
one felt no fear anymore. Or at that level, he asked, did one
still experience a degree of lower emotion?

U.C: RELAXING INTO TRUTH

'Thank you, Jules, for your really lovely words. I can feel
and experience a much more peaceful and relaxed 'you'
tonight. A heavy weight has gone from the area of your left
shoulder.

'You ask me if I experience fear still – or am I able to relax
into Truth with a capital 'T'? The answer is 'yes' on both
counts. I do experience fear, you know – at least, threads of it
are still running around. It is fear of letting people down, of

not making myself clear, of not getting the message of Peace and Love across to the world you live in. We share similar experiences of 'relaxing into truth'. I think it comes through the dawning realisation that, however things may appear to the contrary, one is alright, one is safe, one can be oneself because one is 'at Home'. In your home, which you have made together, you have created a safe haven for relaxation. As you have discovered certain truths during our last few months together, so *they* have appeared like a haven for you to trust and relax in.

'You can be true to yourself because I think you have realised that this salient fact is one of the main pointers for growth. I, in my turn, can also relax as a benediction of love and forgiveness flows over me.

'As Christmas approaches again on earth, and human hearts are more open and receptive, many of us take this opportunity to draw near to earth, to encourage every good, kindly, positive thought that is sent forth.

'Good-night.'

6ᵗʰ DECEMBER, 1989 – Unknown Communicator
Jules deduced that growing beyond fear was obviously a very gradual process – U.C's remarks making him seem closer to us. It was the 'benediction of love and forgiveness' he wanted to ask about. Was this 'forgiveness' *for* something might he ask, or was it rather a sense of rays flooding him whose quality was intrinsically that of automatic forgiveness? Also, since I had suffered emotional turmoil today over the continuation of dictation – 'kicking against the pricks' of routine again –

Jules thought U.C. might have something to say; that is, if I had not already asked, or maybe he had not been aware of the upset. Had Jules created the confinement by sticking too closely and for too long to the routine originally suggested by our Group?

U.C: SOME SALUTARY COMMENTS!

'You are quite right of course when you say that the benediction of love and forgiveness described last time came from one of the Rays – and it is freely available to all. There are no such words here as saint or sinner – just 'God's children'; because compared with Him that is what we are – just children. But no one need feel ashamed, feel the need to hide his face, however unworthy he feels. One is deeply, truly loved for oneself. On earth this is much more difficult to fully grasp because often love and forgiveness seem a long way away. The 'haven' I speak of is nevertheless as much yours as mine.

'Yes, I do know of the problem you have been discussing over the past hour or so. No, Jules, you have not created the confining routine.

'The problem is Ann's sudden awakening to her own vulnerability. She thought herself as having outgrown the kind of feelings that have been running amok in her this evening. She has been having a real tussle with herself. She is tired and far from well, but she must try to find her own Way to freedom. She finds it hard to write about herself and doesn't want to, but I will try to persevere. As I have just said, the routine you have is far from confining, since you can both choose how you wish to spend your time with us.

'Ann seems to have got hold of the idea that the afternoon before each session must be spent like a wake. No need for this at all. Once again, you are both free to choose what you want to do, but she has been using the time lately to fight some old fears and bogeys, which will not seem to lie down or go away. And why is she so hungry? She hasn't got to fast beforehand! She is very adaptable and can easily switch in to me at any time she likes. She doesn't always have to transcribe; she can just sit and reflect if she wants to. I hope these words have been of some help.

'Good-night.'

10ᵗʰ DECEMBER, 1989 – Unknown Communicator
Jules thanked U.C. for his effort to convey his understanding of my problem. It had provided a more practical perspective on the situation – those touches of humour not being lost on us either. Also, U.C's first paragraph had much interest for Jules, an emotional significance that he wanted to read over and over. This was mainly due to his difficulty in self-forgiveness. For if he had put a foot on 'The Way' at all, it was daily making him ever more aware of his faults, more conscience-stricken over mistakes in behaviour, rashness, impetuosity etc. – the guilt reaction to which was quite searing at times. As a possible antidote he tried to imagine that love from the Source, which U.C. and the Group must feel in order for them to want to share it so much – just as he, Jules, wanted to share mere knowledge. Anyway, all that U.C. had shared was highly valued.

U.C.   On Leaving Behind The 'Small You'

'Thank you for the kind words you have just spoken, Jules. I will try to share your experience as much as I can, try to explain what is happening to you – indeed to you both – when the need arises. You are quite right; I do want to share this feeling of love and forgiveness that I spoke of last time, in much the same way as you wanted to share knowledge with all whom you came into contact. I understand that feeling so well. It creates an avalanche of emotions, of ideas and how they can best be put across; of creativity, and of excitement when a response is evoked.

'As you are growing, your consciousness acutely developing, it leaves you feeling raw and naked – worrying about every seeming fault, real or imaginary. It is a painful time to be living through, and yet positive. It shows maturity of purpose, the leaving behind of adolescence, the beginnings of leaving behind the 'small you'. But as you teeter about, seeming to lurch from one emotion to another all too quickly, you are nevertheless learning fast. It is so, so hard to live in the moment, but I do think you are learning to live a day at a time.

'It has taken Ann longer to reach this stage than you, because her daily life up to now has consisted of having to look ahead; or at least it has appeared thus to her. You know, you two are so lucky to be living together. As you love and forgive each other's little weaknesses, so you experience a tiny measure of the Father's great love and forgiveness for you – the love and forgiveness I am privileged to experience, the love and forgiveness that helps an unhappy man, when bowed under the burden of self-mortification, to hold his head up, to feel his way toward his place in the Creator's scheme. Everyone has a place. The whole of Creation is a most intricate pattern into which everything, everyone fits.

'Good-night.'

13ᵗʰ DECEMBER,1989 – Unknown Communicator

Jules said that U. C. obviously well understood about the need to share and the pain of seeing faults. Jules certainly did 'teeter about' etc., in view of which he felt very surprised and encouraged to hear that he was 'nevertheless learning fast'.

It was a later statement that he had been studying closely though, the: 'As you love and forgive each other's faults, so you experience a tiny measure of the Father's love and forgiveness.' Jules asked himself whether he really did love and forgive, or did he basically just endure and forget, as it seemed to him. If so, he could not yet experience even 'a tiny measure'. Maybe, however, as one can become aware of self-hidden psychological beliefs, one can also by awareness uncover this 'Father's love and forgiveness'. Is *that* pouring in anyway and discoverable at the same level, whatever one's limitations? Secondly, does the pattern of creation referred to include events?

U.C: SQUEEZING OUT THE DROSS

'I think, a couple of dictations back, I used the expression that in our world 'there are no saints or sinners, just God's children'. So whether you have tremendous belief and insight, or have no belief at all and are in seeming ignorance of God's great love, it still pours over each and every one. You ask if love and forgiveness happens in spite of how you appear in your own eyes, and the answer to this is, of course, an unqualified 'Yes'. You also say that you are not sure if you truly love and forgive the weaknesses of others in your daily life, that perhaps all you are experiencing is a reduction in irritation until it is called up to the surface again. I say to you that I see the 'inner you', and I can say that you are experiencing these emotions, i.e. love and forgiveness, as truly as you are able. I am now referring to the daily interplay that takes place between Ann and yourself. She in her turn loves and forgives you, so you can help to build and replenish each other's auras. If you can do it for each other, therefore, perhaps you can see what I mean when I say that you experience a little of the Father's love for you. It flows out like a great river, covering each and every one – those who love Him and those who revile Him and curse His name. How often, too, His name is used in blasphemy rather than in love.

'To turn to your second question, Jules. Yes, every event has its place in the great pattern of Creation, as does everyone. You see what are regarded as mistakes, as disasters, as terrible events – these are transmuted as they rise through the levels, rather like being squeezed through a giant press.

The dross is left behind and only the good intent, and the goodness that has come about through the good intent, remain. So they slip easily into the pattern. Like a jigsaw puzzle there is a right place for every piece to be slotted into, however strange the shape. And the whole puzzle, once complete, looks perfect. Indeed, you can't see the odd shapes that went up to make the whole. Many events in human terms seem mindlessly cruel; there seems to be suffering on a terrible scale. It is good to speak out where you see a wrong, good to try to correct it, because in so doing you help to lessen the amount of dross that has to be squeezed out before the goodness that is in the seeming injustice can rise to its correct level.

'Good-night.'

17th DECEMBER, 1989 – Unknown Communicator
Jules was very pleased with both of U.C's answers. (He had had an inkling from me incidentally that U.C. was at times concerned about getting over sufficient answers when two questions were involved, so now he assured U.C. that only one question or theme would be brought up at each session). A close study of U.C's first answer had opened a door of understanding however – one which Jules had been technically aware of, but not heartfully appreciated. 'The penny had dropped' as never before, he thought, in that whatever degree of love and forgiveness he experienced, *this* was the *actual* 'tiny measure of love and forgiveness from God' *brought through him*, or anybody else. It was the *very same 'substance'*. Also, looking in the mirror, he had reminded himself more deeply that here was the lower model of a larger Self, kept securely within It – and the heart's appreciation of this was an extraordinarily safe one, albeit for a few moments. Did this 'love and forgiveness' flow through *only* via the Higher Self, as a possible beginning of contact? If not, perhaps U.C. could correct?

U.C: ANOTHER DIMENSION TO LIFE

'No, you are not at all wrong, Jules. You are absolutely right when you say that your Higher Self is 'bringing through' the Father's love.

The Higher Self glows, shimmers with the Absolute radiance of love, and even he, I may add, is just a reflection of the true glory of love.

'Now in many people the Higher Self can evoke no response. It is like a light shining on a completely dark and shuttered room. The light is there but the person *inside* the room cannot see it. He may refuse to acknowledge its presence, or he may just be blankly unaware of its existence. Whatever may be the case the light continues to shine. Then one day something happens to slightly open one of the shutters. A little of the light filters through and the personality feels strangely warmed by it. He notices that a depth of feeling is added to whatever he or she is thinking or doing. This of course begins to add another dimension to his apparently aimless life. He likes the feeling – as you said, it gives a sense of security, a feeling that you are not alone. It helps the personality to look at familiar objects, familiar events, familiar people or animals in an unfamiliar way. A crust of indifference begins to break up and a real feeling of compassion starts to develop; not false sentimentality but real compassion.

'Now the Higher Self is wise. He knows not to rush things. He knows that the shutters can only come down slowly or the light would be too intense and the personality would bang them shut again. He encourages the personality to do much of the work for itself. I know you must have often met people who are at different stages of development. Some feel cold and repelling – here the shutters are shut. Some have a little warmth in them, but often it is just for a cause or project that has caught their attention; here the shutters are beginning to open. Some seem to 'blow hot and cold' on you – here the shutters are banging back and forth. Then there are some who feel so warm, so comforting, so loving to be with, that you bask in the sunshine of their smile. Here the shutters are fully open.

'This is when the Higher Self is able to bring through the Father's love, and it spreads out in a wide, rippling pool. So I know that your Higher Self rejoices that the 'penny has dropped' as you describe it. You are learning to trust this feeling more and more.

'Good-night.'

20ᵗʰ DECEMBER, 1989 – Unknown Communicator
Jules thanked U.C. and proceeded to go over several parts of his answer to make sure he had understood correctly. He wanted to ensure, for example, of U.C. meaning that the same love being transmitted from the Source was that which the Higher Self *and the lower self in turn brought through* in their own degrees. If correct, there was no need for U.C. to comment. Tonight however, Jules was concerned about 'false sentimentality'. Was this referring to sentimentality as being false in general, or to a particular kind of sentimentality? What, in U.C.'s terms, was being seen as 'sentimentality' compared with 'real compassion', for instance?

There was an unusual pause. (Here I am going to take up

the description of what was happening in my own words). The pause seemed to last about a couple of minutes, the pen remaining still. U.C. then took the decision to try experimentally 'overshadowing' me for the first time. He began dictating at a steady pace but I realised that he was particularly concerned that this following passage should be clear and concise – that it should make good sense. He paid careful attention to the punctuation and began to speak out loud: 'Comma there… no, go back… a dash here… semi-colon here… and full stop'… etc.

U.C:

'False sentimentality is, for example, when people keep their pets 'alive' long past the time when they should have left their physical bodies behind. False sentimentality keeps, or tries to keep, people 'alive' on support machines when these should have been switched off. There is no difference between sentimentality and false sentimentality; it is a false emotion. Period. It only exists in the lower levels of feeling. It is not felt where it should be felt – in the heart. The heart center is dispassionate, calm, dignified. The heart center feels – no, 'feels' is not the right word – it IS love and compassion… love and compassion directed to the very center of the person it wishes to help. The heart center, when opened, is most practical, most hard working. It does not waste time looking back at what might have been, or how sad something is.

'It gets on with the job it was created for – which is channelling the love of the Higher Self and, by that very inference, the love of the Father to those in need in a most workmanlike way. In this way false emotions do not get tangled up in it. It knows exactly the area of a person's psyche that can benefit. It does not matter who that person is, or what he or she may or may not have done – the channelled love from the Father will unequivocally restore and strengthen weaker areas of another's aura.

'That is love and compassion, and that is the difference between it and sentimentality. You have to be able to look beyond the personality, which you may or may not know, and recognise the child of God who is standing there clothed in whatever persona he or she has chosen to adopt. I hope this explains it a little to you. I have put it in rather simple terms, I know.

'Good-night.' (vocally whispered through me).

When I re-earthed, as it were, I explained to Jules what had happened, and also told him this after-thought left in my mind by U.C:

'Sentimentality is a form of greed nurtured by the personality who wants to hold onto something it thinks to be of value, whereas real compassion is very workmanlike.'

24ʰ DECEMBER, 1989 – Unknown Communicator
Jules said a special Christmas prayer in welcome and blessing. Then, after a reflective moment or two, he remarked that U.C's answer last time about 'sentimentality' could not have been more clear. He felt particularly appreciative too, on this seasonal night, of all that U.C. and the Group had brought

into our lives – what had been lovingly given through the months, apart from everything else, in the form of an opportunity to look inside and grow. The only difficult theme in U.C's answer was that of seeing 'the child of God' in everyone. Again, was the head's imagination a good start when nothing was felt deep down? This he had tried with very slight success, though the attempt had been riddled with current indecision and self-enquiry over past relationships in the mind – whether to cut off altogether or at least treat these mental cameos with a more realistic perspective.

Knowing that I had a question, he wished all a Happy Christmas, praying they may find in the New Year more of what each could uniquely do to bring the love they felt through to others.

U.C:

'Thank you once again for your thoughtful words, Jules. I know you pick them with extreme care, too! Yes, the imagination can be a most enormous aid to development, however hard it is to see the child of God, standing in front, masked by the features of someone you don't particularly care for. But don't turn anyone away, even though the association may seem futile and useless. People come and go through one's life, weaving in and out like a long thread. Like threads, the association can become frayed, and may even snap of its own accord. Don't be the one to pull too hard on it. To carry on with the analogy, each thread has a beginning and an end, so an association will quite naturally finish. If forcibly broken however, it may become necessary to take up certain 'unfinished business' in the next incarnation. Much valuable time for development can be wasted in this way. That is why we, who see a little more broadly, always encourage those of you on earth never to let an opportunity for forgiveness to pass you by.

'I have so much enjoyed these past few months too, Jules. After all, you have given *me* an opportunity to do what I like best – wagging my tongue at length! Seriously, if I have helped in any way at all then I am glad. Our association will continue. May the peace and quiet blessings of Christmas be with you tonight. I know the Group send their Happy Greetings too.

Before Jules came in for the session, I had privately asked U.C. about a strange experience I had twice encountered recently. From somewhere in or around my bedroom the sound of a woman crying had been heard. I thought it must be a woman because of the particular tone and manner of the sound. No normal physical cause could be discovered. Jules and I live alone and the adjoining house is empty. Cats are often heard, but this was a human noise.

Then, once, I was aware of it much closer, much clearer. Someone was invisibly snuggling into my back while I was lying in bed. I felt the face quite distinctly rest itself on the nape of my neck, 'till it faded away.

I prayed for the person, whoever it may be, and tonight sought an answer from U.C.

'Now Ann, you ask me about the crying you have twice heard on waking. This is a woman, a discarnate, who is in the greatest need but we are unable to reach her; so she has been

114

guided to you. She clings to you like a child, and I know you give her all the warmth you can. She is known to you, but I won't tell you now who it is. She will come to you again.'

(U.C. went on to comment about other problems I was undergoing connected with my prayer work, private life, and the Parkinson's disease).★

'Try, if you can, to be calm about the ups and downs you are having. You are carrying great burdens for others, so of course you feel stressed. Your inner development is progressing quickly and Simon (my guide) is working closely with you. But because you are rather buffeted, another Being of radiance is helping him. This Being has great experience of working with dedicated sensitives. His name is Norinus. Call on him at any time.

'And do get plenty of rest and drink – I would suggest *lots* of milk. Our blessings to you too this Christmas Eve. You have been a faithful scribe for me, and I am grateful. But remember, you *can* cope with all that seems to be flung at you nowadays. Inwardly you are strong and balanced. We would never have chosen you if you hadn't been.

'Good-night.'

27th DECEMBER, 1989 – Unknown Communicator
Jules said he valued the repeat confirmation that what he could imagine helped the climb toward actual feeling in his

---

★Actually, Jules had found me collapsed on the floor earlier, summoned from his room by my tapping feebly on the base of my bedroom door. He helped me to my feet, a prayer was said, and he returned for the time being to his study.

heart. He ran over U.C's text, acknowledging the felt rightness in his answer about 'associations'.

He was surprised that U.C. actually enjoyed the sessions, which came as something of a guilt-relief, liking the idea that it gave U.C. an opportunity to do what pleased him. When it came to forgiveness however, Jules said that he found this much too difficult at present. Looking inside, as U.C. had originally suggested, Jules thought he saw an ego that would feel itself let down by forgiving felt wrongs. So pride looked to be very much the culprit. 'Is that basically what it is, do you think?' he asked.

U.C: FORGIVING OTHERS

'Yes, Jules, it is pride. Now, you said that perhaps you could not forgive many people in your life because in so doing you feel you would be letting yourself down. I think I have quoted you correctly. I say back to you that you are letting yourself down by *not* forgiving. These words sound harsh, and to forgive others for wrongs done to one is extremely hard for most people to do. But you know, like most things that seem hard to begin with, once you have done it the first time, it becomes much easier the next time, and so on.

'Think back a bit too. The person who was slighted, wronged, i.e. yourself, is a very different person from the one sitting in this room tonight – very different. After all, you change from day to day. Growth *does* fluctuate, but as I said to you not long ago – once started it cannot be stopped. And you *have* grown. I have watched you grow over these past months. So here we have you, a different person. The person who was hurt has largely disappeared you know. Oh, you may not think so, but you have. The people who slighted you – they too have changed. Nobody can stay exactly the same. So the hurt hangs between two different people; it has shrunk in proportion. Only your thoughts about it can give it shape and size. Take your thoughts off it and it shrinks. It has nothing to do, in reality, with the person you have become – only if you let it. In a way, you don't have to do anything other than not think about the hurt. This is not forgiveness in the highest meaning of that beautiful word, but it is a start. Full forgiveness may or may not follow.

'You seem surprised that I have enjoyed these dictations, but I can assure you I have. I said jokingly that it has given me an opportunity to wag my tongue at length!

'That is what I used to do when last on earth. Oh yes, I know now that I loved the sound of my own voice, and did indeed say much more than was really necessary. Most of us do. Economy with words, to make them *matter*, is difficult. Within these dictations I have to get several points across in a disciplined way, within a time limit. This is all to the good, because if my dictations are published then hopefully people will gain knowledge, and above all comfort, from them. This is why it is good to keep them short, because most people can only *really* absorb a little at a time. But you know, sometimes just a phrase can alter the whole way of thinking for someone.

'Good-night.'

31ˢᵗ DECEMBER, 1989 – Unknown Communicator
Jules said an appropriate prayer for the Group and all those

whom they tried to help including the newly re-born countries like Romania.

He then agreed with U.C. about 'economy with words' and getting points across 'a little at a time'. This made teachings far easier to absorb. He took U.C's point too about letting himself down by *not* forgiving. The rest that was said encouraged him. But when he tried to sense what was behind the pride, all he seemed to find was turmoil – a mess inside, which the pride was attempting to defend, he thought. And the prospect of forgiving 'X' (someone mentioned) looked impossible from a position of weakness. He couldn't forgive others when he hadn't first forgiven himself. He also felt rather silly when U.C. must have suffered such tremendous earthly injustice with far more to forgive, of a degree that made Jules' own whining look pathetic. He recognised in his head the truth, the rightness of U.C's words, but from below as it were, the stomach was shouting: 'No! I can't!'

U.C: DISCARDING UNWANTED 'JUNK'

'Jules, thank you for your frankness and honesty. One thing I just wanted to say first of all – and please bear with me a moment. You say that you know with your head the attitude you should take towards forgiveness, but that your stomach won't seem to let you.

'Once the heart has opened a little it will be easier, because this will help you to get your emotions out into the open.

'Now, down to practicalities. You say that you feel 'a mess' inside, and cannot see how you have grown. The 'mess', as you describe it, is all the old unwanted thoughts, feelings etc., being sloughed off as so much dross. The personality is very churned up at the moment, not sure quite what to try to rid itself of first. One thing: this forgiveness of 'X' you mention. For the moment, leave it at what I discussed with you in the last dictation. Just try to take your thoughts away from the subject and leave it at that for the time being. Forget about whatever I may or may not have had to forgive when last on earth; I chose it all in advance, and from my experience can try to help others like yourself. So don't feel silly. No need for that.

'This 'mess' you feel is, as I say, the dross being chucked out. It is like having to wade through garbage in the streets before you can reach the pleasanter atmosphere of the park. Or clearing out the house for a jumble sale – you look at the pile of junk mounting in the hallway and wonder that it ever had anything to do with the life you are leading now. But as the house junk is carted off out of your life to the sale, so the same thing is happening to your personality right now. I see behind what you call the 'mess', and see the new you – the one I talked about who has grown – standing there. But you have to decide what you want to discard, and what you want to hang onto. Only you can do the sifting. What I, and others like me can do, once you have decided what you want to dispense with, is help you remove it. That is no problem for us.

'Well, a New Year and a new decade dawn tonight. Countries are wanting change just as you are, and many of us are busy helping them. They do need all the prayers you can send. May I wish you both a year of inner growth and stability.

'Good-night.'

LETTING GO

3rd JANUARY, 1990 – Unknown Communicator
What U.C. said last time had been helpful to Jules who emphasised the accuracy of certain descriptive sentences about his present state.

'Anxiety and relaxing down from it' was the theme tonight, he said, 'a common human need'. Into it, of course, came worries over my increasing Parkinson's symptoms, and the effort to deepen faith. He described his memory as a child at Christmas, gazing up in wonder at the Christmas tree, feeling utterly secure and relaxed in his Sussex country home. Was U.C's sense of the 'love of the Father' anything like that? Did he also feel, over or through frustrations and frictions in human life, that all was *really* well, all of the time? Jules then went on to describe what he thought might be, at last, his impression of the inner self coming in: (1) Occasionally, for about fifteen seconds, and very sporadic, the experience of sudden, deep relaxation – the influx of a certain attitude. (2) Quite separately, that of someone or something with a very strong, calm, curious empathy for physical textures and neatness. Was this at all significant? And would U.C. like to comment on the theme?

U.C: BECOMING AWARE OF THE BLUEPRINT

'Yes, the love of the Father does help me to relax down from anxiety, but if I may I'll come back to this in a moment.

'First let me say that I rejoice to hear you describe the feeling that comes from within – a feeling that helps you relax, if only for a few seconds, a feeling that is aware of the textures and designs of your world. As perhaps you may have guessed by now, I am leading up to say that this is the 'blueprint' of the new you that we have discussed before – the person waiting in the wings. As you become daily more aware of him, so your periods of sudden, complete relaxation will be extended. And as I also said a while back in the dictations, you have to go on living in this world – so your new 'persona' is getting used to the feel of the world around. You are clearing a pathway for him by beginning to discard some of the dross. You are dropping old, stale ideas and associations, and this gives him a chance to 'merge' more and more with you. The clearer your thinking, the higher you strive to reach, the more you manage to control your lower emotions – then the more you will begin to feel at ease with this new persona. As I said to you last week, you have travelled fast in these few months and are an eager pupil. Good!

'Now, back to my opening remarks. I like your story about your childhood and how secure you felt. Often children are unaware of the love of their parents; they take it for granted. They do become aware, however, when this love is not there. They feel insecure. So it is with people who are unaware of the love of the Father for them. They feel insecure too, frantically rushing around trying to find this love, but often sadly only finding a cheap imitation. Yes, I am very, very conscious of the Father's love for me. Your experience of standing under the Christmas tree as a small boy is like being in this light. Everything is right, everything has meaning, everything has depth, everything is forgiven because this love takes all one's sorrows and anxieties. I do still experience these feelings, you know. But as my burdens are lifted from my shoulders, so I want to do the same for others. Love is forever in bloom. Its essential essence is eternal. Everybody returns in the end to savour the sweetness of its perfume – they are irresistibly drawn despite themselves.

'I know you are worried about Ann, and I know she is having a very hard time at the moment. It may well get tougher for her, but she has enormous faith and this will carry her through. One of us is constantly with her, and your love, too, supports her. It is what we all need, wherever we are – to love and be loved in return.

'Good-night.'

7th JANUARY, 1990 – Unknown Communicator
Jules was at once gratified and interested in U.C's confirmation that the inner experience he'd been having was indeed the blueprint, though he had not experienced this for the past couple of days. However, a key sentence thought Jules was the one beginning: 'The clearer your thinking…' all of which seemed to boil down to in-depth practical living, since the lower emotions primarily hurt oneself. And the phrase: 'This love takes all one's sorrows, anxieties…' reminded Jules of the enigmatic Christian belief in Jesus'

supposed sacrifice on the cross, even if it didn't happen physically. Why couldn't they say what they mean? Anyway, what exactly in us was blocking this 'love'?

Mystical experience of it, in Oneness, had been apparently experienced by a wide spectrum of average-seeming people, as evidenced by Sir Alister Hardy's collations. Would Jules' 'blueprint' bring through something of this?

U.C: MATCHING UP TO THE 'BLUEPRINT'

'Yes, Jules, the love we have been talking about will be felt by you to a greater degree than you do now, by the new 'blueprint', the new you. The love is there, always has been there, always will be there. But you have been blocking it by operating most of the time – not all the time I hasten to add – through the lower emotions. Now you are dissatisfied with yourself. I know we have discussed this before, but it is important. You have reached this crucial, new stage in your development, in your evolvement, where you want to step out of yourself. You say that you have not felt glimpses, experiences of the new you, for the past couple of days. Don't be concerned at all by that. You are doing a good deal of mental sorting, thinking hard about what to discard – not wanting to be too hasty. While you are busy concentrating on your old personality, you cannot expect to experience the new. Your new maturity is helping you to make the right decisions. Each right decision made will help you to match up to him. I agree with you – clear thinking is practicality.

(Pause) 'I understand from David that the skin on your hands is sore and cracking. This to me is symbolic of the eruption going on in you at deeper levels. The old skin is being sloughed off, the surface is cracking – rather like a volcano cracking the earth's crust with its secret inner fire.

'The Master Jesus died symbolically on the cross – the cross, of course, representing the figure of a human: head, arms and legs. With His symbolic death He took the burdens of mankind into Himself, and always will. Mankind can, in turn, if evolved enough, carry the burdens of lesser-evolved brethren. Hence the story in the Bible of a man stepping forward from the crowd to help carry the heavy cross under which Jesus was laboring. It is a story rich in symbolism. In this case the man was prepared to risk punishment in order to help his Master.

'But this is evolution – humans gradually learning to care about others before themselves; a steep, stony road, yet one which leads to freedom and forgiveness.

'The people you mention who experience feelings of love, light, oneness etc., have for a time been dissociating themselves from their physical bodies and have 'tapped into' the eternal fount of love – the love which is ever in bloom.

'Good-night.'

Jules had also said that it never occurred to him that his sense of security in childhood was due to the love of his parents. He had always assumed that it was the child's freedom from responsibility, the cosy environment etc. As an after thought now, U.C. communicated that the love of the parents created both these factors.

10ᵀᴴ JANUARY, 1990 – Unknown Communicator
Jules felt much consoled by U.C's answer, which had 'made sense'. The business of change seemed so slow (he thought because he was not making enough effort), especially when ordinary social interaction showed up the same behaviour in 'this silly personality', he said, with a note of irritation. He did, however, see all nature as being welded together by love, yet, at the same time, in constant renewal, from the cells in our bodies to the chrysalid of a butterfly, to even himself trying to shed the old perhaps, and to those who shed the need for physical birth altogether. Meanwhile there was confusion, frustration, indecision with anxiety as to the right use of free will, and thence the need sometimes to 'reach up inside' wordlessly in appeal to some 'Highest Being', whether imageless or clothed as an archetypal figure. The little ego wanted to stretch higher than its Overself at such times, Jules noticed, though probably that was where the energy reached. So in U.C's observation discarnately, how valid or effective did he see this stretching, albeit momentarily, could be for the average human without sectarian leanings? When he felt so little love, could he reach and draw justifiably?

U.C: CHANGE HAPPENS GRADUALLY

'Yes, oh yes Jules, do ask for help. Your cry, your call, your prayer *will* be heard. Even I do not really know quite how the process works; I only know that it does. Indeed, discarnate helpers are often sorrowful that they are not approached more when their earthly charges are in trouble. Only when it appears that a really 'tight spot' has come are they occasionally called upon.

'Of course, in this time of transition from the old personality to the new, you are beset with anxiety, fear, frustration etc. I can so well understand the frustration because I always wanted change to happen quickly, immediately. But if you look around you at nature, changes there happen gradually, gently. The seasons merge slowly into one another, until in the end you can't quite pinpoint when, say autumn changed to winter. You simply know that one day you are using the phrase 'now it is winter' instead of 'now it is autumn'.

'In the same way changes are taking place in you – and I promise you that they are. But just as sometimes there are dramatic weather conditions while one season gives way to another, so dramas are also being worked out in you. Your old personality is confused and fearful. You appear to drop a certain way of thinking and the way seems clear for your new personality to get 'the feel of the water'. The old personality then becomes unsure, and bangs a door in his face. But the new one is winning. Don't doubt that for a moment. Trust me. And what is much more important, trust in the Father's love for you. Become as a little child. Hold out your hand trustingly when times seem bleak, and when you are far from loving yourself, let alone anyone else. He will take your hand and help you along the steep, stony Path of which I spoke. His love is always there, and to those who ask He will more than gladly give.

'Therefore, do not feel inhibited to whisper a prayer for

help. I only hope that this hasn't sounded too much like a Christian sermon! Many folk are put off by such phrases as 'eternal life', imagining endless days in a kind of vacuum stretched out in front of them. Yet 'eternal life' means Life with a capital 'L' – meaningful, loving, purposeful, full of zest.

Let me end this dictation by saying that you do know inwardly when you have made a right decision, just as you know when you have let yourself down. Keep in good heart, Jules.

'Good-night.'

14th JANUARY, 1990 – Unknown Communicator
Before Jules arrived, U.C. told me that this was going to be an important evening. He knew that Jules was feeling 'emotion', and he wished to help him extend this. There had been a buzz in the room for about ten minutes prior to eight o'clock when Jules was due.

Jules came in and after the usual prayer wanted first to reassure U.C. that his last answer had not sounded like a Christian sermon. From an earthly priest it might have done, but from a discarnate such as he, it was assumed to be from direct mystical experience and thus respected. Having been quite meaningful, the answer had in fact drawn out emotion from Jules. He had tried to read it with the 'feeling' side of his nature, and both this and the words had helped him to peek inside himself at the hidden emotional beliefs suddenly seen to have been restraining his energy in prayer. These were: (1) That the emotions must be largely suppressed because they made him vulnerable. (2) In result, the lack of emotion so curbed his initial private approach to prayer that he believed any attempt or effort lacked the power to reach far enough. The belief contradicted head-knowledge, but he suspected many others felt the same, deep down. (3) Guilt that he was not making enough effort plus a sense of unworthiness where his problems were felt to be too paltry for high attention, only strengthened the further belief that in order to grow spiritually he must needs struggle on his own, mostly without help. 'How could one begin to overcome all this?' he asked in forlorn tones.

U.C:

'Yes, Jules, I know you have felt held back, constrained for a long, long time – and I am trying gently to lead you to the place in your own heart where the floodgates that bind you so tightly can be slowly opened. If we do this together you will not feel so vulnerable, so raw.

'You have enclosed yourself in a belief, a feeling that if you keep everything you believe firmly in the head, using your intellect to examine it closely, then you are on dry ground. But you need to get your feet wet a little. You need to feel a rush of emotion. This will be very cleansing for you. Now, you say that your prayers will hardly reach to where the High Being is. But you do not have to 'reach up' because He is all around you – and of course not just you, but quite simply everyone. You are quite right when you state that many feel just as you do. They sense no one. They feel alone. How then can anyone 'out there' hear them, let alone answer them? It is one of the reasons why I want my dictations published, why

I stress over and over again – and I make no apologies for so doing – that no one is ever left alone, however terrible the burden they carry, however unworthy they feel.

'How can this be so?' – people will ask. God is talked of as some exalted Being, way up on high, seated on a throne. But I say to you that He is in the very air you breathe. He *is* the very air you breathe. It is hard, so hard, to put this into words. How can I explain it? It is as if your planet and all the planets and the galaxies are held in the womb of the Creator. As a mother is aware of the movements of her dear baby within her womb, even though she is busy with matters of her own, so it is with the Creator. He is aware of every movement, every struggle for existence, every cry for help, however faint at first that cry may be. If only I could help people to realise how personal God is to them – not far away but intimate and loving – it would help to open hearts. By opening our hearts, by becoming aware of the feelings of others, emotions rush from us like God's love being spread on an outgoing breath.

'Good-night.'

17th JANUARY, 1990 – Unknown Communicator

Jules had been touched by U.C's second paragraph; also willing but nervous at being so led. However, what particularly struck him was the enormous difference between head-knowledge and emotional superstitions underneath. Headwise he knew perfectly well that God's spark of light was in every atom of substance or air all around; moreover that our whole galaxy was atoms and cells in the physical body of

All That Is. Even what little he sensed from the heart had always confirmed this. Yet his primitive 'stomach' attitude, of whose beliefs he'd just become aware, had been left wallowing far behind. The observation clued into U.C's specifying of what looked like a still deeper, unfound belief in him – the *need* to keep everything in the head. Now, U.C's last sentence puzzled him. Did this mean (he said half-jokingly) that he had to become aware of, for example, the grocer's feelings before needed emotions would rush out?

U.C:

'Your emotions, Jules, do need to escape from you. But you do not have to be aware of the feelings of others *first*. Rather the other way round. As you and I move together off your 'dry ground' – out of your head in other words, and into your heart – so the block that is causing trouble for you will begin to shift. As it does so, you will become aware of what went to compose it, and you will feel some pain. You cannot make this step without feeling pain, and I know that you hate discomfort! But I also know you well enough by now to state that you will put up with almost anything if you see the point.

'To recap: we have moved off dry ground, and you are starting to get your feet wet. As you begin to feel emotion, *then* you will be much more aware of others' feelings. I realise that I'm jumping you forward what must appear like several stages, but once the block has been removed, you will move more easily, breathe more easily, feel more easily. Therefore, your outgoing breath will be full of these new, fresh sensations, breathing out will be an outpouring of God's love.

As you have just said, you have the metaphysical head-knowledge. Intellectually you realise that God's love isn't 'up there', but is in the air you breathe. So you breathe it out. You are doing it now, but are emotionally unaware of it. I realise it is hard for someone like yourself to even begin to know the feeling, but it will happen. *This I can assure you.*

'Good-night.'

Downstairs earlier, I had an experience partly witnessed by Jules seated on an adjacent settee.

For about an hour that afternoon I had been reading a book by Dr. Maurice Nicoll, a devoted follower of Gurdjieff. Dr. Nicoll had been explaining how we seem to repeat the same life over and over again, making the same mistakes, appearing to get nowhere.

While agreeing with this worthy gentleman, I promptly fell asleep for about half an hour. On waking, I felt strongly dissociated. The sitting room grew slowly dimmer until familiar objects looked distant, as if seen through a smoke screen. Large wings were flapping around my head, further obscuring my views of the physical world. I sat still and waited. 'Somebody' had arrived whom I sensed shared very strong connections with me. He wanted to speak, eventually saying: 'EDVER VI SOLUM MAICRUM.' He repeated this phrase two or three times. Then he blended away, and I returned.

Puzzled by the whole extraordinary incident to say the least, I was impatient to seek an explanation from U.C. His answer came as a complete surprise.

U.C:

'Ann, you were relaxed and contemplative this afternoon, and so were afforded a glimpse that is rare for many – that of your most important former life. In years as you would measure them the life took place about 100 B.C., but in another solar system, quite unknown to your scientists of course. There on the planet, which is called 'MAICRUM', you learnt the arts of healing, prayer, and love in its most pure and highest sense.

'You tell me that he said: 'EDVER VI.' This means: 'I come in love.' 'VI' means: 'I come' – 'EDVER' means: 'in love'. Those of you on earth now, who have placed your life at our feet in order to be of service to your fellow man, all stemmed from the Planet Maicrum. Then the switch was made to Planet Earth so that through incarnations there, you could gradually develop the skills you learnt on Maicrum, to be used where they are most needed.

'You had been reading Dr. Nicoll where he talks about former lives and how we seem to repeat the same old pattern over and over again. Yes, one does. But at the same time that you are repeating weak points so you are forging the good, strong points. Gradually, these latter outstrip the former. You also mention the wings. These would have been symbolic, and simply emphasised the shutting off from one world while you slipped into another. As you know, you are there all the time; you have never, of course, left. Your self *there* helps you with the prayer work.

'You don't need me to tell you that this dictation is most sacred. God's blessings to you, child.'

21st JANUARY, 1990 – Unknown Communicator

Jules said that U.C's explanation had been perfectly clear, reassuring, and correct in the belief that pain would be tolerated if the point was seen. He went on to remark how he was becoming aware of his surface self being trapped behind a veneer of unreality to which it was also clinging. He knew it was unreal for he had seen over and under it. But it seemed like a sheet of glass, which, although by habit he usually looked *through*, he could not look *at* in itself. Now U.C. had said that as the 'block' shifts one would become aware of what went to compose it. So is one supposed to shift the thing by self-awareness, or must it shift somehow of its own accord before one can see what it is and be freed? Slightly confused re the point of self-awareness, Jules was agitated, stuttering. He finally hoped U.C. would 'get the drift' of this garbled question!

U.C: THE OUTER REFLECTION OF A CORE BELIEF

'Yes, Jules, I did get the drift all right! The tension in you is so near the surface now that it is causing your thoughts to race madly around. The main cause of this tension is your feeling of unworthiness. It may seem contradictory to say that the tension is near the surface and yet at the same time deep-seated – very deep-seated; but this is the case. As this deep-seated belief – this core belief in your feelings of guilt about events either tackled in the wrong way or not at all – rises to the forefront of your consciousness, it is beginning to crack up and send out sparks of anxieties all over the place. For example, you were telling me the other week of your anxiety in just getting on a bus.

'Your head-knowledge has provided you with security up

to now. You were sure of your metaphysical facts, keen to share the knowledge with others – but drew back from transferring it down to the heart. So, as you have matured you have begun to realise that something is missing. Suddenly all this head-knowledge alone doesn't seem to add up to much. As the feeling became stronger in you, the core belief – which has its roots spread over many previous lives – began to make you feel decidedly uncomfortable.

'You say that you feel as if you are trapped behind a sheet of glass. This 'sheet of glass' is an outer reflection of your core belief, which has held you prisoner for a long time. You know that the 'new you' is on the other side of that core belief, but are not at all sure quite how to reach him. This is why I say we will do it together. To shatter the belief and thereby the glass suddenly, would be too painful. We have to prise it away with care. I suspect a number of conflicting emotions are running through you at present. Let them run. Be they anger, sorrow, joy, exasperation, guilt, pride – whatever they are, let them come. That is what *you* have to do. Only you can do that for yourself. What *I* can do is help you shoulder them, transmute them. This is what I meant about transferring from the head to the heart. You are moving out of the head, experiencing emotions with what you would call the 'stomach'. I will help transmute them, and center them in your heart.

'Once the 'glass screen' is removed, the old you will be ready to face the 'new you'. This meeting can take place gradually. The transition will not be a sudden one. In the world of love everything is smooth and graceful.

'Good-night.'

CONFLICTS

24ᵗʰ JANUARY, 1990 – Unknown Communicator
In the hour or so before session time, all that which had been smouldering within me for a couple of months now rose to the surface: the incapacity caused by the Parkinson's, which limited my active life, the resentment over fixed periods of communing accompanied by the consequent guilt, were all expressed to Jules. There was reluctance to attend tonight. However, I knew how privileged we were to receive such personal attention and warmth from one such as U.C. Of course, I couldn't refuse to be his scribe. However, when Jules came in, I handed him a note expressing those feelings, which I wanted him to read out loud.

He first acknowledged U.C's last answer saying he had understood, then he read as requested from my notes:

'Why do I feel so fearful? What do I think I have to be afraid of? I know I am resenting having to undergo this fixed discipline as I see it. I hate the feeling of ill-health hanging over me, and feel that without it I could be doing so many things. I have also been struggling for some time now with the guilt caused by not really wanting to be 'the scribe' anymore. I realise too that you know this which, of course, adds to my

135

guilt. These statements sound pathetic, but I simply have to express them.'

My eyes were filled with tears, making it almost impossible to see the pad and pen as I waited to record U.C's response.

U.C:

'At last, child, I have some comments from you. I have been expecting them for some time, and will bring you what comfort and help I can.

'You state that you feel fearful, and wonder what it is that causes this. You too are very close now to stepping into the skin of the new you, as I have been discussing with Jules. The fact that your former self from Maicrum was able to speak through you last week is a strong indication of that. So your personality in this life is beating with angry fists at the changes – the old you fears the clarity, the open-mindedness of the new you. But you know in your heart that you have nothing to fear.

'The question of becoming dependent upon others through ill-health I will answer next. Yes, your body may or may not become dependent for its everyday needs. But your mind, your spirit *will not*; that is your own, running free. Of course you resent ill-health. Anyone who is normal in their mind would, and one for whom you help carry the burden is very ill at present. He needs a lot of help, and this is further adding to your difficulties. You have also been helping with rescue work during sleep, and I think it would be wise to desist from that for a time. It will be arranged.

'Now to the thorny problem of discipline! You quite

naturally feel resentful that, after thirty years of looking after others, you seem to have further restrictions put upon you. But these are largely of your own making. You are imposing far too rigid rules on yourself. I think you are expecting to be an angel in human form – you are damming back far too many emotions, trying too hard to be perfect. Let yourself go much more. You are also trying too hard at the very painful job of digging out all your past mistakes, as you see them. Leave these alone. *BE* in the present. This way you can watch the change from old to new taking place.

'You say you could do so much more if you were free from the Parkinson's disease. I say back to you that you can do so much more *with* it – which leads me to the question of your mediumship, acting as my scribe. Yes, I have been aware that for the past three or four weeks you have been reluctant. I know that you have been working for us over the past eight or so years. Can I just say, simply, that your gift is a rare one, valuable beyond price. I know that it is difficult to set your own thoughts to one side, but the work we are all doing together will live on to change lives. I will say no more now – just that we love and understand you. *You* are a pilgrim. You have known inwardly from birth what your destiny would be. I touch your hand as a brother.

'Jules, I am glad that my last dictation has been of some help. We have begun the work together already. We will speak again.

'Good-night.'

28ᵗʰ JANUARY, 1990 – Unknown Communicator

Jules again expressed his appreciation of what U.C. had said to us these last two sessions. It helped in the daily struggle to find the way to 'live life aright'. Indeed, this seemed the only worthwhile purpose, and not a day went by when he didn't at some time wince at his own stale attitude, despairing of its repeated failures. One sentence of U.C's had particularly rung true the more he considered it, i.e. that the main cause of his tension was his feeling of unworthiness.

So how, when one is born ultimately from the goodness and love of the Source, does one *contract* this disease of unworthiness? Do many people do so? And do they experience this 'hell'? What about the 'man in the street'? But then, even Lawrence had said once that he felt 'unworthy' to be a guide, and if *he* still felt unworthy, what hope was there for someone like Jules?

U.C:

'Do you know that children's game that they often play with their parents – that game when Ma or Pa stands behind the child, and the child leans back further and further until they drop into the parents' arms? You will know what I am getting at. As adults we lose the trust, the absolute trust which comes from knowing that no harm will ever really befall us. No obstacle will ever be placed in our way that is too difficult to surmount, no pains too great to bear.

'As an adult, Jules, you have lost a lot of the simple trust, not only in a Power greater than yourself, but also in your own judgement. And this loss has created confusion, tension in you. You ask if many people go through the hell you are experiencing? I answer in the majority, no, because they have never really bothered to think very deeply about the Creator and His Creation. In the main, they are busy building a material nest around themselves – cars, holidays, parties, or maybe their job has become all-important. Now, if these things were suddenly taken away from them, then they would feel bereft. For some it might mean a new beginning, however.

'You are not much interested in materialistic things, I believe. But you have spent most of your adult life in an *intellectual* search for the truth. Having satisfied your intellect that it certainly exists, that there *is* a God shall we say, you suddenly feel out on a limb. Here you are not alone. Countless people have been at this very point, encountered this self-same dilemma. How does one fall back into the Father's arms? What I think you find hard to trust is your head-knowledge that you are worthy of His attention. And even more difficult is how to express and live the higher emotions when the lower ones seem to be always getting in the way.

'This causes the conflict, the confusion, the daily tussle with yourself. You *will* gain mastery over these lower emotions, I promise you.

'Primitive man – and many in the world today are primitive men – did not suffer this conflict, for he trusted in his own body, his sympathy with nature. He lifted his eyes to the sky in worship of his idols, but he questioned very little.

'Perfected man does not feel this conflict because he has learned to live in his higher bodies. In-between man, if I may call you that, does feel conflict. He feels unworthy as you do. I said that this unworthiness has its roots spread over many lives. This is because you arrive with the 'blueprint' but drift away from it. Inwardly you have been aware of this fact. In your present incarnation, much about your real psyche has been revealed to you; again you know inwardly what is to be done. You are aware that many are helping you, and this serves to increase the sense of unworthiness.

'Take heart, my dear friend. Your struggles are helping to shrug off the old skin. I am aware of your deep distress and share in it with you. Try to remember that you are a child of God, and trust in that.

'Good-night.'

31ˢᵗ JANUARY, 1990 – Unknown Communicator

BEFORE THE SESSION:

U.C. arrived early with Margaret, and so I took the opportunity to ask him a question that had been puzzling me for some time. This stemmed from the fact that when I prayed for folk whom I did not know, their guides on request rushed toward me with ideas for help. But whenever I prayed for Jules I appeared to meet with a blank wall, which friends of ours had also encountered when trying to send him absent healing.

Moreover, I felt absolutely no response at all from his guide, David Wood. So what was the problem with Jules?

U.C:

'You *do* help him. As you know, no prayer ever goes unheeded,

140

no good thought is deflected. And therefore ways are shown you to give him comfort. But you two are closely entwined – you *have* been through many lives. However, it is deemed best that not too much is revealed about the inner self of the other. Much that is sacred has become known about each of you, but *that* much and no more! David does listen, nevertheless, when you pray for Jules.'

After taking this dictation I sent out a prayer of healing for the atmosphere of Jules's room, imagining the room full of a blue, cleansing light.

Suddenly the atmosphere in my own room changed dramatically! Two or three minutes later I 'knew' that an invisible intruder had appeared on the scene, and that it was my old adversary nicknamed 'Cyril'. I am accustomed by now to his restless movements, and have come to recognise them. The little portable bed-table, which I use to write upon, was in place on my lap, the clipboard and pen resting on it as always. Without warning my right wrist was being held fast, the clipboard and pen pushed onto the floor. In defence I sent out the strongest thoughts of love I could muster. He ignored these and pushed me forward in the chair, trying to throw the small table on the floor. I held on to this with my left hand, determined that he shouldn't have things all his own way.

Jules came in then, ready for the session. Seeing me slumped forward in my chair he realised something was amiss. Although not quite sure what, he gently eased me upright by the shoulders and stood behind with his hands still on them, praying. I, in turn, tried to continue sending thoughts of love to Cyril, who had broken away and was prowling restlessly round the room.

When Jules considered matters comparatively settled, he took his seat and, after the usual prayer with an amendment for the occasion, started to comment on last session's dictation.

He said that U.C. had been absolutely correct in all that was surmised about him, and that a surge of emotion had even been felt at such elder-brotherly understanding. The theme however was: 'What is to be done?' Was this some unconscious secret he was keeping from himself? And indeed, 'how to fall back into the Father's arms?' – a question, he supposed, like 'how to fall in love?'; it just happens.

But he wanted to tell U.C. that an hour ago in his study, he had again been subject to a neighbour's boy revving his motorbike below the window, which normally caused great irritation. This time he decided not to be irritated but to remain passive – keeping the noise apart, outside. It worked straight away, and he saw how unnecessarily we hurt ourselves. Did U.C. think that this was what Dr. Nicoll meant by: 'a man must learn to become passive to himself'? And isn't this passiveness to emotion contradictory to U.C's advice to let it all out?

(When the moment came to start dictating for U.C., the intruder Cyril had begun trying to grip my hand, and several anxious minutes passed before I managed to move it at all. Slowly I got the better of him, although over the first sentence or two writing was most difficult. But then, at last, there was a 'whoosh' of feeling and Cyril was gone. I knew that U.C.

was present beside me all the time this was happening, and I was also aware that he felt I was quite capable of dealing with the situation on my own. However, my writing was small and cramped to begin with, then flowed back into its usual style).

U.C:

'The incident in your study which you describe, being passive to the noise of the motorbike, is exactly what Dr. Nicoll means with regard to being passive to yourself. The 'inner you' decided that he was not interested in the world outside him – he had no concern with it. His attention was turning inward, and the outer world scarcely impinged upon what he was doing or thinking at that moment. I said, a couple of dictations ago, that it is good to express emotions, to let them out – but only if you feel the need to do so at that time. From the description you have given me – and no, it was not mundane at all, but important – you sound as if you were not having to make a supreme effort to control irritation; it just happened spontaneously that you were passive. Afterwards, probably, you felt much more comfortable, more at ease than you normally would have done if tension had mounted. Thereby you got a glimpse of how comfortable life on earth could be if you were always passive. But I reiterate that it has to be a genuine experience of non-emotion, non-feeling.

'Now, to turn to trusting in the Father's love for you. This has to arrive spontaneously too. As you say, it is a little like 'falling in love' – one day you aren't, then suddenly you are. It seems inexplicable. So it is inexplicable to describe being aware of love for the Father, and aware of His for you. It simply comes into one's everyday life.

'To return to the subject of emotions for a moment. You can freely give rein to your emotions yet still remain passive. *You* are in control of them. You feel, you experience but at the same time you have a stillness deep down inside you.

'Now I will stop here as Ann has been having a battle. She has won. I purposefully did not interfere because she needed to feel she could make it on her own.

'Good-night.'

4th FEBRUARY, 1990 – Unknown Communicator
Jules opened with a humorous comment that perhaps Cyril's obstructive behaviour was a protest at my calling him 'Cyril' – though he did not mean to make fun of what was a difficult experience for me, and understood U.C's stated position. He felt that U.C. had clarified much, and went on to confirm for him the reaction of spontaneous 'passivity', in which there did seem no effort. He then expressed his yearning for that 'stillness' inside, which he seemed to have lost over the years, if he ever had it at all. And was the 'inner' part to which U.C. referred actually the 'blueprint' due to take over? Was that 'blueprint', furthermore, holding the 'stillness'? Jules' feeling to get out of the old casing had become pretty well a need, a hunger now. But was he on the right track in these questions?

U.C: UNCOVERING THE 'BLUEPRINT'
'Yes, you are absolutely on the right track. This center of stillness I mentioned, this quiet, secret place deep down inside

you is the 'blueprint' we have been discussing. I don't know if it would help at all, but you may imagine this 'blueprint' as being in the region of your physical heart, very quiet and still. For the moment the rest of you is *not* quiet and still – far from it! It is restless, swinging from one mood to another, nerves jangling and twitching, longing at times I think to scream at the world and other people. But he is there, your 'blueprint', and if you can make a conscious effort to calm the outer you, then he will have a chance to grow. His serenity, his calmness, his dignity will fill your outer self.

'We will try the well-used analogy of the overcoat. Take the overcoat as being the 'you' that is experienced every day at present. It feels tight, rather ill-fitting, shabby in places that you would prefer not to see. Then imagine the overcoat without you inside it. You are so fed up with the feel of it that you have decided to discard it altogether. Then watch your body fill with the 'new you'. With the old you now gone, he has his chance to fill the outer skin. The body begins to take on a new demeanour, or coat. This looks different altogether. It is no longer ill-fitting or shabby, but looks like something from Fifth Avenue, or Bond Street. The passiveness has spread and grown to fill every fibre of you – your blood, your nerve cells, your muscles. They are in good working order, but not concerned with reaction to outer events – only with responding and synchronising with your Higher Self.

"This all sounds beyond me at the moment," I hear you cry. Yet daily exercise of the type you described in the episode of the motorbike will allow such passive stillness to spread through you. As you agreed, no effort seemed necessary on your part. It isn't. You simply have to allow it to happen. You know he is there. You know how different you could be. You know how different you desperately want to be. Indeed, you accurately described it as a daily need, a hunger. Now is the time to assuage that hunger.

'Good-night.'

7ᵗʰ FEBRUARY, 1990 – Unknown Communicator
Jules was particularly pleased with the answer U.C. had given. What had to be done was quite clear, and he hoped that one day others could benefit. Equally remarkable was the fact that again, although Jules himself had never got on with specific techniques involving visualisation, those which U.C. suggested were the kind he could do, indeed *was* doing.

It left him clear of personal questions, but he wondered whether the present climate of political change in Eastern Europe, the Soviet Union, South Africa and elsewhere could be compared to the individual's change in accordance with a blueprint. And as now the prevailing freak storms and floods were taking their toll, with 80 m.p.h. winds gusting outside our window even while he spoke, was this also symptomatic of a tide for change in the world? (This may not be as far-fetched as it sounds, for discarnate teaching has described in detail how our inner, psychic, world climate affects the outer one). He thought perhaps U.C. might like to comment.

U.C.
'Yes, I would very much. We here of course greatly welcome the massive radical changes taking place throughout

the world. Nations have their 'blueprints' just as people. Nations that have become rigid and fixed need to shrug off their overcoats, their old, worn-out ideologies and beliefs, their tyrannies by the few over the many. All this needs to be discarded, for the new coat is waiting. Men of vision are showing themselves on the world stage while despots lose their hold on power; men like Mikhail Gorbachov who have waited patiently in the wings for the right moment to step forward. A man like him, a sensitive, articulate man, would have had to witness many horrors and injustices before his moment came to fulfill his destiny. As he set the chains loose in the rest of Eastern Europe, he knew that the flood-gates which had dammed back reform for so long would have to be opened.

'Of course I welcome the changes in South Africa too, but here the differences go much deeper. Within Russia you see communism fast breaking up, yet that has only been powerful for seventy odd years. The black man has been made to feel the inferior of the white man for much, much longer than that. The black man is a volatile creature, and centuries of resentment have to be lifted from him before the 'blueprint' of such countries as Africa and America can be fully adopted. Oh, there are still small pockets of potential trouble too in countries where men become excitable in the name of religion – Iran and Iraq for example.

'There are many countries where human suffering is great. But the differences caused by language, governmental style, or religions are beginning to lessen. Now, it is important for the more phlegmatic countries of Western

Europe to stay calm, offering the hand of friendship to those latterly thought of as enemies. The West feels uneasy and turbulent in emotion, hence your bouts of severe weather.

'Over the next decade, a man of immense strength and beauty will emerge from where he has been waiting in the shadows, and greatly help to unify planet Earth. As I said recently, many of us are staying close to Earth to help her through this period in her long history. Men and women are moving closer together, and universal recognition of the Father will take place. It matters not how he is recognised, only that love takes its rightful place again, reigning in all human hearts. Man the Pilgrim has begun his journey.

'Here now, for a while, I will bid you farewell. We will all meet again on the first Sunday in April. You have both reached a stage where you must work alone. A break from the sessions is called for. It will give you an opportunity to explore inwardly. But do not fear. We will not be far away, and I shall look forward to taking up these dictations again in April. Have faith, my two pilgrims on the Path.

'Good-night.'

RESOLUTIONS

Over roughly nine years of twice-weekly sessions, of sitting together, even when the Group chose not to come through, such a break was unprecedented for us. It felt strange. However, the spur to inner development, prayer, and loyalty to our invisible friends, coupled with a sense of routine, still drew us to our rooms at around the same time twice a week – a time when we were each aware of their silent companionship.

Nothing unusual occurred during the ensuing two months, except that I began to notice an increase in my Parkinson's symptoms. Whether or not these were due to a discovered over-prescribing of drugs we did not know. Severe fatigue and nausea took their toll to such a degree that I began to think I would never again be the 'scribe' for U.C.

Somewhat ironic, thought I ruefully, remembering 'kicking against the pricks' not so very long ago. Now I wanted to help him more than ever. But as the days grew longer with the approach of April, I found something of my former vigour returning.

1st APRIL, 1990 – Unknown Communicator

Spring was in the air all around us, and this evening Jules and I were in a state of anticipation, withdrawing to our rooms around 7 p.m. I had a good deal of prayer work and therefore welcomed the presence and assistance of Curator, my Guide, when she arrived half an hour later. Tears came into my eyes and a lump rose in my throat on realising that she was accompanied by U.C.

Jules entered for the usual 8 p.m. start. He gave the prayer, and warmly welcomed back anyone who was present. Originally he had intended to ask U.C. what he had been doing in the interim – helping with the profound changes that had affected Europe maybe?

But a personal insight had caught his attention, the result of stepping back inside himself to observe his own present feelings, reactions to the new start. He came out with this almost immediately – the fact that the small mind or ego felt itself as a pupil returned to school guilty that it had not done enough homework. He observed it wanting change because of its own psychological discomfort and not through any altruism. Most of all, and ironically, he saw that the change wanted by it, as from the swallowing of a simple pill, was not realised to involve its own 'death' so to speak. 'Who,' he asked, 'is the observer here?' Certainly 'he' seemed to be someone who was after growth for its own sake rather than to escape discomfort, someone who was tired of a false ego masquerading on his behalf, though whose attempts to break the pattern were overclouded by his ego's superficial inclinations. Anyway, if anyone felt like

150

commenting or not, there it was. It felt good to be with them again, he said.

U.C. was just about to start dictating when Jules spoke again: 'I'm sorry to interrupt, but with a shock I have just belatedly realised my own self-centredness in forgetting to ask how you are. And I was going to say how much better Ann had been feeling etc.'

(Through me U.C. put out a hand and gave Jules a comforting pat on the shoulder).

U.C.

'Welcome to you too, Jules, after our break. I have been busy on the world scene. Much has been happening as you know and much more is going to happen in the year ahead.

'Now I know that you and Ann have kept vigil on your own and I felt that to be a good idea. It has given you both time for reflection in your different ways, a time for reappraisal and reassessment. I have been dictating at some length since last July, and I welcome the fact that the scripts are being put into book form. Ann has not been at all well for a while and I applaud her efforts at 'keeping on, keeping on'. An appraisal has been necessary on my side too, as I know the typing of the notes has been difficult for her at times. What I have decided therefore, with your approval, is this. We all meet together every fourth Sunday from this one, (Ann will know when it is), and you can either ask questions, Jules, or if you feel there is nothing in particular you wish to ask at that time, then I shall simply dictate in the normal way. This way I can still provide material for the book but at a slower pace.

'Ann can still be used as a channel during her prayer time, and you, Jules, may benefit from the opportunity of being freed from the onus of having to ask a question!

'You said at the beginning that you were using tonight to stand back and watch the small mind at work but you were not sure who was doing the observing. I can tell you that it is the 'blueprint' who is the observer. How hard it is for us to detach ourselves from all the games and tricks that the small mind loves to play. One just has to be firm – to clamp down without shutting down. Your time on your own gives David a chance to be with you. I don't know if you have been aware of his guiding hand?

'Earth at the moment seems like a giant volcano – so much hot, spewing lava is being thrown out. Once the crust of indifference, intolerance, ingratitude, indecisiveness and indignity has been gently prised away, such a healing of old wounds will be able to take place. Soothing balm will be able to be applied by all of us who love you in your struggles – your struggles to break free from the mould. Love is very much at work and in evidence.

'I understood your interruption. You were not being selfish but expressing your feelings as you have been asked to do. Ann is better again I know, and in that fact I rejoice. You have both been struggling in your individual ways. I give you into God's care and protection and I will be back.

'Good-night.'

29th APRIL, 1990 – Unknown Communicator
U.C. arrived early, told me his theme was going to be

152

'Lanterns' and asked me to write in this title. Jules then came in, gave the welcoming prayer, and said that he and I were both very happy with the new arrangement. Trying still to become more conscious of his true feelings, he noted that the real reason for his 'sitting here' was one of loyalty in supporting the conveyance of U.C's point of view to the world – a motive which, though mild in appearance, was full of emotion and somewhat redeeming to his sadness and confusion at general lack of inner progress. When sitting alone these past weeks he had felt a 'presence' each time, but was unsure of late what inner stance to adopt. He had tried on occasions to sincerely lift up his heart to the conceived source of All That Is, of pure love and creative goodness, straining in desire to grow to Its highest potential within him. Was this in fact a practical, effective thing for anybody to do, or was it an unrealistic endeavour at this stage? He hoped the question did not intrude on any theme of U.C's.

U.C: LANTERNS

'You must have guessed my theme for tonight, Jules. What you describe as a 'lifting of the heart' in aspiration is indeed of tremendous use, not only for yourself but for many others. I see your 'lifting of the heart' as a turning up of the wick in a lantern. This enables the light to burn more brightly so that other travellers on the Path can see it as a welcome. The world needs many lanterns to form a circle around the globe.

The light from one lantern can share its glow with another, can add to the light from another lantern so that the beam can stretch further into the darkness. Many at present are living in a darkness of their own making. On the surface all may appear fine, but inwardly there is only shadow. If a light from a lantern held high by one endeavouring to serve the Lord of Light can fall across them, then a little of their inner darkness can be dispelled. Perhaps you can see from this that your time alone is not wasted.

'We who love you are lucky to have so many of you on Earth whose dearest wish is to help us in our work. Every nation, every country, has servers of mankind living quietly among those who hold out their hands of help. Some of the servers live humble, simple lives, some are busy with the grind of commerce and industry, some are materially wealthy; most you would never suspect of being a server. Until, that is, the lantern of one burns out in a sudden, iridescent blaze of light and, ah then, you recognise he or she. The one sure rock-like certainty is that the lanterns can never *ever* be extinguished on earth, however terrible the circumstances may appear. They are handed on as a lantern bearer returns to us, and more and more are being lit. One day everyone will carry one, even if only dimly lit; but, for the moment, that time seems distant.

'It is fellowship indeed to be with you both again tonight, and you are both benefiting from working alone between times. We shall meet again four weeks from this evening, and we all send our warmest blessings to you. You are both beginning to stand on your own two feet, even if you feel unsteady at times. Hold your lanterns with pride.

'Good-night.'

27ᵗʰ MAY, 1990 – Unknown Communicator

Jules prayed in earnest thanks for the company of our unseen friends and for the wonderful knowledge of their presence with us. His prayer also conceived how their invisible work behind the scenes must often be thankless and go unappreciated by those helped, so he asked a special blessing on them. U.C. was then welcomed personally.

Jules reported that I had been unusually well* over the weeks, for whatever reason, though he himself had been sitting alone feeling rather hopeless confronted by seemingly endless character faults and not being able to trace the tangled web of attitudes behind them. The twin principles of 'love' and 'self-awareness' were obviously major keys to growth. But because the latter was difficult, to say the least, he had been wondering if real loving, passive behaviour was being overlooked as a solution *in itself* to the unravelling of one's faults. The oft-repeated dictum of teachers to 'love' sounded a bit too demanding a notion to 'Everyman', whereas gentle self-discipline simply towards more 'loving behaviour' looked first a closer step, and second, a possible solvent to the 'glue' which stuck tangled attitudes so fast within a person. He imagined U.C. might like to comment.

---

*As luck would have it, after weeks of feeling so much better, this particular day the Parkinson's had been very troublesome and I was sitting in my chair prior to the session feeling somewhat sorry for myself. However, U.C. arrived and the tremor stopped immediately. It was rather like a skin being peeled off one's arm. I was made whole again.

U.C: TO GIVE THANKS FOR THE CREATOR'S LOVE

'First of all, a welcome, a very loving welcome to you both and thank you for keeping our appointment. You notice I have underlined the word 'loving' to emphasise its great importance. It is perhaps the most over used and yet (in its truest sense) little understood word in any language known to mankind. 'I love you. Do you love me?' 'I love my new car, new dress' etc. But if you take a moment or two, and it need only be a moment or two, to dwell – I won't say meditate – to dwell on what love in its highest sense really means, then its beauty and humbleness will move you almost to tears. To dwell on the theme that the Creator, the Lord of all Light, created each and every one of you out of Love, is to move, albeit seeming so slowly, back to this love.

'You probably feel that you have moved out of the circumference of that love, but if you can spend a few moments every day giving thanks for Him from whom you sprang, then you hold in your hands, in your heart, the key to unlock your tension. You gave thanks in your prayer tonight and a lightness, a feeling of peace, surrounded you. If one had nothing materially, maybe even simply the clothes one was wearing, and yet could still give thanks for one's very existence, how rich, how warm, how blessed one would be. Most people feel starved of this so essential food; they search for it everywhere and know no peace. We love them and try to heal and fill their empty hearts. So let that emotion which urges you to be grateful well up and flow out. It doesn't have to be directed towards anyone or anything – it can just happen.

'I am glad that Ann is well and strong. I think she has

found a key to her problems; but she must still be careful not to overdo things as she discovered today. We will meet four weeks from tonight. Enjoy the summer days.

'Good-night.'

14/15ᵗʰ JUNE, 1990
Jules and I had been to our local town on the 14ᵗʰ for half a day or so, meandering round the shops in a leisurely fashion, having coffee, then lunch. Nothing particularly strenuous. On arrival home Jules looked drained. His face was white and beads of perspiration were evident on his upper lip. He lay down on the bed and fell asleep. I was puzzled and rather disturbed by all this as I knew that such mild activities should not exhaust a man of forty-two. Was he seriously ill, I wondered?

Before I went to sleep that night I asked if the Group could give me an explanation or tell me how to help him. I drifted into a dreamlike experience where Jules was brought to stand in front of me; I knew it was him although the skin on his face looked extra soft, there was no facial hair, and his eyes looked smaller. I was asked to touch his face, which felt as delicate as a baby's, and I was also asked to kiss his cheeks to help encourage healing. This I did.

Upon waking I heard an inner voice telling me that as Jules felt he had no identity at the present time, his nerve endings were exposed and consequently he felt raw and tense. He wasn't 'earthed' for the time being. Therefore, having no real sense of identity or personality, he had no structure to lean back on as a cushion. This made him feel insecure and somewhat unsafe, so tension had built up resulting in tiredness and headaches etc. His eyes appeared smaller because everything about his old personality was shrinking.

I was also told that people with strong, outgoing earth personalities had a good deal of physical vitality because this is where their energies are concentrated. Introverted people like Jules, who need to know where they stand, need to feel secure, would suffer quite acutely during any changeover period.

1ˢᵗ JULY, 1990 – Unknown Communicator
U.C. had told me some months ago that I had agreed, before incarnating, to carry on my shoulders the burden of Parkinson's borne for two weaker members of our Group, thereby freeing them for their development. This information had been deeply troubling me for quite a while, and his early arrival gave me the chance to slip in a couple of questions:

'Because I am "carrying a burden for others", U.C., does that necessarily mean that I must carry it for the rest of my earthly life? Can't I in fact overcome and dissolve it myself?'

U.C:
'Yes, you can overcome and dissolve it yourself. You will have to concentrate very hard to do this but if you can imagine the three of you walking easily and freely, untrammelled by anything other than a feeling of the radiance of God's love for you all, you may find it easier to achieve. If you can constantly remind yourself that you are always in the circle of this love

and try to extend that circle to permanently include O. and P., then that is all you need to do. There is no burden then to carry, only love to be put into practice.'

Jules came in at that point, and said he sensed someone present, and although not quite sure if U.C. was there, offered apologies from both of us as we had missed the agreed date. (We should have held the session on the previous Sunday.)

He said he had tried to 'dwell on what love in its highest sense really means' as U.C. had suggested. He had thought about the fineness and gentleness of nature's appearance, the sea and the hills, the soft grass and trees – recognising that such intrinsic beauty could only come out of Love's pure rays condensing into these features. Any ugliness was either man-made or man's distorted conception. Moreover, if one thought of love fashioning all nature, it was difficult to conceive the possibility of anything lower entering into that energy; the fullness of it would be too great, it seemed. But, especially since he felt a bit like a mistake on two legs at present, the way he had interpreted U.C's suggestion could be mistaken. Was this the sort of 'dwelling upon' which U.C. meant, thanks for which could give rise to a release of tension?

U.C:

'I have just been speaking to Ann about love, so I will gladly continue for you, Jules.

'Love as you say is in all nature – gentle and eternal – and yet at the same time it is a powerhouse. The tension in you is also a powerhouse. The two energies, which both spring from the eternal Source, are in conflict – rather like crossed wires that give out unpleasant shocks. But faulty wiring can be corrected so that light and warmth are constant and not in imminent danger of plunging the house into darkness.

'You are energy. You are the energy that created you, the energy from which you sprang. However, this energy has become static – rather as if you can't loosen a faulty plug. For a while you need to do nothing, feel nothing, be nobody. Explore this non-feeling, try to catch a glimpse here and there of what *really* matters to you, what is of most importance to you, where your values *really* lie. Try to exist in this state of non-being for a day or two.

'We who love you can help to 'carry out the repairs' so that when you 'plug into the world again' so to speak, you will be thinking and acting along correct lines and Love in its highest sense will have a chance to manifest through you. Something has to alter in you, I feel; you want this to happen too, I sense that. I know this to be a most fervent wish.

'Apologies accepted, of course. You have both had a testing time since we last met but I would like these dictations to continue every four weeks. It is important for Ann to be used as a channel.

'Good-night.'

AN INNER STILLNESS

22nd JULY, 1990 – Unknown Communicator

Jules began lightly by saying that he hoped we had got the date right this time. He then affirmed that U.C's suggestion to 'feel nothing, be nobody etc., for a while' was felt to be right. Inside, he had sensed a prompting to let go somehow, but it was not formulated, and U.C. had supplied this. Although Jules had not fully succeeded in letting go, he would try again. Now he detailed an experience which, in view of all U.C. had said through the months, seemed worth reporting.

'I had walked down to the sea alone one afternoon; alone except for bustling tourists, that is. I had taken no drugs and had made no unusual suggestions to myself. As time went by I began to feel more and more 'filled' from within by a welling-up of peace, and utter relaxation, which consumed all fear and anxiety. It was like having taken a strong drug perhaps, yet far more profound in depth. I walked up to a point overlooking the sea. It seemed as if the normally conscious 'I' was just in the eyes and in the slender motivation of where to go, where to look etc. 'I' felt suddenly on the surface, superficial. The rest was occupying three-quarters of my body up to the front. It was just benignly allowing, witnessing through me; very passive, neutral. I cannot say it was a person. Maybe it was no one. It just saturated me with inner stillness. I didn't start loving people, but there was an utter calm acceptance and fearlessness occupying my body that I'd never known.

'It lasted about an hour or two, then gradually wore off by the time I got home. Since then, I've not been able to bring it on again with imagination. What do you think it was?'

Lastly Jules expressed his interest in the fact that U.C's communications, when studied alone, often gave him a sense of the 'Love' of which all teachers spoke. It was hoped this would encourage U.C. for his book.

U.C.

'Jules, welcome. I am sorry you have such a bad cold, exacerbated by the heat, no doubt. Thank you too for your encouraging sentiments.

'Now to turn to your 'awakening' experience. You asked me what I thought it was and I can say that the description fits the person 'waiting in the wings'. The peace welling up from within, the feeling of security and fearlessness, all point to this fact. Very encouraging that the sensation, the depth of feeling, lasted for nearly two hours – this indicates to me that your attempts to follow out the method I outlined last time have paid dividends! Please do not be discouraged in any way if you haven't been able to recapture the experience; I can guess you're longing to; and how elusive it must seem; and perhaps how empty you have felt since. But as you say it just happened spontaneously (it cannot of course be forced), and having happened once it *will* occur again.

'What you have longed for – the blueprint we have discussed – has been given the right conditions to manifest himself through you. You freely allowed the personality you have worn all these years to stand aside. You have touched a little of the heights, therefore don't be saddened if the depths seem more than a little murky. They will clear again. You are also throwing out waste material along with your cold.

'I think I know you well enough by now to realise that you won't strain after the experience. Lead as normal and contented an everyday life as possible, while allowing yourself time for reflection and moments of quiet. Allow your heart to hold the special feeling that was evoked that afternoon by the sea; let your heart be a mirror for this 'other you' to be reflected in. You said to me that you did not start to love people and I would have been most surprised if you had immediately done so. As the heart is able to expand, your attitude toward your fellow man will, imperceptibly at first, begin to alter. You will most probably begin to view them more gently. You will almost certainly begin to feel more self assured, and become assertive in the correct way. I rejoice for you and with you. You have earned your reward.

'Yes, you had the right evening! All is well with us and once again I say that I will be with you four weeks hence. I am delighted too that Ann is keeping well. O. and P. are benefiting from your practice of the method I described last time, Ann, as well as yourself.

'Good-night.'

19ᵗʰ AUGUST, 1990 – Unknown Communicator

When U.C. arrived about 7.30 p.m. I had been praying for two suicides known personally to me, and now took the opportunity of expressing to Duncan (a member of our Group accompanying U.C.) how his frankness years earlier about his own suicide had greatly assisted me in this prayer. As he responded and we swopped thoughts on the matter, I became aware that it was easier talking with him than with my guides. The contrast found me turning to U.C.

'I don't understand why I can't seem to feel the presence of Simon, or even Curator, at all easily – and yet I've experienced such a fluent interchange with Duncan. Why is this, U.C.?'

'Child, it is because they are almost too close to you. It is often difficult to speak to those nearest to us, especially if we suspect that that person knows us inside out. Adolescents often find it easier to talk over a personal problem with a trusted member of their family, but *not* their parents. They feel too intimately involved and it can cause constraint. So it is with one's guide. Quite frequently you can feel awkward in their presence, feel they might be wondering why you haven't 'done better'.

It is quite possible to keep personal thoughts hidden from them; they know your emotional body but the personality often likes to distort or keep hidden – often very deep down indeed – certain emotive feelings. It plays games as we have mentioned before. It is less than sincere with itself so it is difficult for the guide to unravel the great knotted ball of string, which often passes for human thought, to get at the facts. Be as careful as you can to keep your thoughts clear, concise and truthful. If you want to speak to Simon be totally open and honest with him. Hold nothing back. He needs a complete picture of a problem to enable him to give advice, if that is what you seek. Try to remember this, child.

Jules came in as U.C. was finishing the last but one line. U.C. paused there, and listened to Jules' prayer for the Iraq-Arab situation. This emphasised a white light of good intent within the hearts of all involved on the borders, that it might increase into their minds and soothe everyone towards a peaceful settlement. After welcoming U.C. and Duncan, he said that no unusual developments had taken place during the month, and that although he had thought of a question there was the customary anxiety nowadays about taking up time that U.C. might need for planned dictation of his own – on the Iraq crisis, for instance. However, the question tonight was on behalf of an imaginary 'Everyman', who did not have our opportunity of contact yet who felt encouraged to sit alone for half an hour or so, quietly trying to feel the presence of his guide. The inclination to prayer may not be strong, lasting only a few minutes; meditation may seem far out of his reach. How could he best spend his time in the company of his unseen guide, a time he earnestly wanted to be helpful to both. Thinking loving thoughts towards his fellow man, perhaps? If so, what else?

U.C:

'Now, good evening to you, Jules. I won't speak on world events tonight except to say that many of us are being kept busy at the moment in that part of the world. Prayers such as yours this evening are welcomed by us; they really do aid us in our work at reconciliation, at increasing the strength of the Love ray. The Iraqi leader needs to feel loved. He is such an unhappy, fearful man. He needs unconditional love however he appears to behave.

'As you will see I have been talking about guides tonight with Ann. You, as 'Everyman', sit alone in your room with your guide and ask the question many of course do ask: 'How can I best be of help?' The empty vessel is of the most use. The empty mind, the empty heart – empty but eager to be filled with love. This is a tall order, as empty places have a habit of being filled with unwanted guests. However, if you can keep your thoughts as free as possible from daily worries and, yes, think lovingly of anyone you know whom you feel would benefit, this can be a very profitable way to spend the time. Fifteen to twenty minutes will probably be as much as you can manage to start with. Then, maybe, listen to music that holds a particular deep, spiritual significance for you. The music will help to lift your mind, will aid relaxation, will give peace and tranquillity. These feelings, these emotions will help to build your spiritual strengths. Once you have built some spiritual strength, you will be much more ready to tackle your earthly problems.

'It has indeed been good to be with you both again. I shall be coming every two weeks for a while but I do not want you to feel pressured into asking questions, unless you *really* want to. Please feel completely free – you know your presence is very welcome.

'Good-night.'

U.C. then went back and finished the last line of his answer to me.

2ⁿᵈ SEPTEMBER, 1990 – Unknown Communicator
Another early arrival of U.C's at around 7.30 p.m., slightly surprised me. After welcoming him I did not ask any questions. However, I think what follows was in answer to my frequent and fervent inner yearning to be of service to the Group. Without any preamble, U.C. asked me to begin taking down dictation and gave the simple heading:

SERVICE

'Yes, Ann, you can be of service in so many, many different ways. You know of the two, O. and P., whom you have especially chosen to help. Well, your continually imagining the three of you walking in an ever-increasing circle of God's love and radiance is being particularly beneficial, but you can draw even closer to O.

'Let me explain. Try to encourage him to use his mind, his talents, in the service of others. He has considerable organisational skills and these can be put to good use; he has an air of authority about him, which encourages others to listen to him. His development will be aided in a way he never ever imagined if he can be encouraged to keep his mind clear and pure. And you can help him with this. Many self-help groups will spring up as a result of the conflict in the Middle East, but groups like these can become too fragmented to be of much use – from experience I know that small groups need to come under a larger umbrella. He could help co-ordinate these. Suggest to him that he change his name if he feels this would help, perhaps to use his middle name – Leonard. If he can be led to see children as individuals with needs and emotions, children perhaps deprived of their fathers, then this should help him to stop seeing them as sex objects with no rights over their own bodies. Try also to encourage him to burn the photographs etc., he may still have. Symbolic I know, but a kind of phoenix rising from the ashes; O. rising and becoming Leonard – someone strong and noble.

'P. is drifting. He needs a firm hand on his shoulder, but we don't expect you to do it all on your own! His guide has the situation well in hand where P. is concerned.

'The other two whom you have been given a chance to help are strong and fairly evolved already. Here you should be able to draw really close and become acutely and accurately aware of their needs without any guidance from me. Try to spend some time each day with them.'

Just as the last sentence was completed Jules entered. After the prayer, which acted on U.C's advice about the Iraqi leader, he said that there was no specific questions tonight – only a feedback on progress. He had been trying to dislodge old 'ghosts' from the mind, and with some slight success. But still there remained a central block of invisible, tension-causing belief he could not get at, let alone shift.

Trying to see it was like groping the air, he said, for self-awareness had not yet gone deep enough. He confirmed U.C's statement (to me) about how awkward one felt in the guide's presence etc. It had made him aware of a *belief* that his guide (David Wood) saw him as unresponsive because of not trying hard enough. So U.C's suggestions had been particularly helpful as a definite pattern to follow. In other respects at least his itching, dry, cracked palms of six years had completely cleared up; his nightmares seemed to have stopped, his stutter had largely disappeared, and tension was fading. He had even succeeded, in spaces of thirty seconds at a time so far, in keeping himself an 'empty vessel', and from it had come a brief intimation of his higher nature – though one he shrunk from trying to verbalise. (I too appeared to be reaping the benefit of U.C's words to me on the first of July. Regular practice of his advice seemed to be having effect. Certainly the Parkinson's was no longer such a burden). Anyway, Jules was thankful for the guidance, and he ended with an 'Over to you now, U.C.'

U.C:

'Strength of purpose, strength of faith, strength in a desire to change, strength to get hold of these elusive beliefs is needed now, Jules. Here comes the hard bit, the more difficult bit I spoke of a while ago. This is the moment when I have to say: 'Over to you' for a while. 'Over' but not 'out', as I will not be deserting you, nor will David, but you have been given a frame – a shape if you like. *You* know the kind of picture of yourself you would like to see within this frame, and you are getting close now, much closer, to the blueprint than you were six months ago. I think one of the most important times came during that experience you related to me, that took place one afternoon while out walking. I think you probably remember vividly what that felt like. Now, if you can slip that feeling, that shape into the empty vessel, even if it is only for thirty seconds or so, then the blueprint will begin to become more and more familiar.

'This transition stage of the old personality giving way to the new has to be done by the pupil on his own; this is sacred between you and your Higher Self. Please do not worry if it all doesn't seem to happen at once. You may feel nothing for a while. But a cleansing, purifying process is taking place as you drop away unwanted, unnecessary loads. Quiet, reflective moments will help you to sense His presence and gently to welcome Him. It is akin to watching a beautiful dawn flooding a landscape with color as the heart begins to open.

'Good-night.'

It seems appropriate to end here. 'Everyman' has perhaps reached a plateau where he can rest for a time before moving on. He has a bewildering array of facts to assimilate.

Paul Beard's book 'Hidden Man' largely concerned itself with the kind of guidance offered by U.C. Mr. Beard mentioned how such guidance may be given to the pupil years in advance of the pupil's actual readiness for it.

'Whether the guide speaks by outer communications through a medium, or by a deepening process of private inner communion, wherein with infinite patience he tries over and over to make an impact upon his pupil, it is like the sunlight caressing a bud until it is no longer too green and tight to open. What he says will perhaps well up into the heart and mind only years later. The help is there, the vision is described, the readiness must be in the pupil.'

This certainly came to be the case with Jules, for not until ten years later did all that U.C. said to him well up into his heart and mind. Only then did Jules truly see its relevance and feel in a readier state to apply it. He and I both hope the fact might be of comfort to others who have struggled here with him, and counsel patience with the self that may as yet be a mere bud.

AIDS TO THE BLUEPRINT

A quick reference guide

- Check thoughts as they arise and win your freedom. If you can start to bite off the harsh words, or check the unpleasant thoughts, you should begin to feel calmer – and this should help trace your limiting beliefs.

- The clearer your thinking, the higher you strive to reach, the more you manage to control your lower emotions – the more you will begin to feel at ease with the new you.

- You clear a pathway for him by beginning to discard some of the dross, dropping old, stale ideas and associations.

- You have to decide what you want to discard or hang onto. Hard to begin with, but as old habits drop away you will feel lighter, fresher; it begins to make sense.

- A cleansing, purifying process is taking place as you drop away unwanted, unnecessary loads.

- Let emotions flow, and the block of tension-trouble will begin to shift. Pain is inevitable.

- Struggles help shrug off the old. You know inwardly what is to be done.

- Quiet, reflective moments will help to sense the blueprint and gently to welcome it.

- Let your heart be a mirror for this 'other you' to be reflected in.

- It is the blueprint who is the observer. So exercise self-observation, and detach yourself from the ego games. Each right decision will help you match up to him.

- Keep your eyes, ears, mind and heart very alert. The more self-awareness is practised, the easier it will be to sense his presence.

- Try to watch yourself relating to others. It is not so much what you express that matters, but what you observe yourself thinking or feeling. From this comes a clearer picture of who you are, and that is important.

- Love the faults in yourself. Accept yourself with failings.

- Acknowledging what you really feel in a naked, harsh light, is an important step; self-acceptance of how you feel from moment to moment.

- Explore and concentrate on your feelings of good intent.

- When you feel ready, begin to ease yourself out of one of your coverings. You will feel lighter, less weighed down. Your Higher Self knows the way.

- Take the overcoat as the 'you' experienced at present: tight and ill-fitting. Then imagine the coat without you inside it. You have discarded it. Then watch your body fill with the new you, a new demeanour. The passiveness has grown to fill every fibre of you – your blood, your nerve-cells, your muscles, with health. They are in good working order now, and strong, but not concerned with reacting to outer events; only with responding to your Higher Self and synchronising. Serenity, calmness, and dignity has filled your outer self.

- Daily exercise of passive detachment will allow such passive stillness to spread.

- Remember that you are a child of God, and trust in that. Sink into the absolute feeling of security, the sense of peace that can give.

- Spend a few moments every day giving thanks for that Love from which you sprang, Step forward in faith.

- Acknowledge to yourself your right for existence, for being; that you are an essential part of creation.

- Live your life as fruitfully and wisely as you can.